the awful thing in the attic

and other scary, true stories of ghosts, strange disappearances, and UFOs

Brad Steiger

1999
Galde Press, Inc.
Lakeville, MN 55044 U.S.A.

First Edition, 1995
Third Printing, 1999

Cover design by Christopher Wells

Printed in Canada

Library of Congress Cataloging-in-Publication Data

Steiger, Brad.
     The awful thing in the attic : and other scary, true stories of
ghosts, strange disappearances, and UFOs / by Brad Steiger. — 1st
ed.
         p.   cm.
     ISBN 1–880090–17–1 (softcover)
     1. Ghosts.   2. Haunted houses.   3. Unidentified flying objects—
Miscellanea.   I. Title.
     BF1461.S8   3   1995
     133.1—dc20   95–15244
                                                                    CIP

Galde Press, Inc.
PO Box 460
Lakeville, Minnesota 55044–0460

contents

introduction:
is your attic haunted?

"It's coming from the attic," the woman told me, trying her best not to allow fear to warp her voice. "All the terrible disturbances are coming from there. There's something awful in the attic."

The house was suffering from an extensive range of haunting phenomena. Doors opened and closed of their own volition. Ghostly sighs and murmurs were heard through the home.

Soon after the family had moved into the house, the dog they had had for seven years ran away and never returned.

The television set and certain other electrical appliances were completely nonfunctional during the hours when the eerie phenomena were most intense.

When I visited the home on a rainy October afternoon, I felt that I had been summoned to the lair of the Demon King. The place was huge, a massive sprawling Victorian mansion that I had been told had been sitting empty for many years. If ever a house looked haunted it certainly was this old manse in northern Illinois. With its tall windows suggesting eyes, its mammoth door, an open mouth, the old house looked as though it were screaming.

According to the letter that I had received requesting my assistance in helping the beleagured family to understand their paranormal problem, the woman had read a number of my books and felt that I might have some arcane formula that would put to rest the eerie phenomena that had so afflicted them. I surely had made no such claims; and I had tried politely, but firmly, to suggest they try elsewhere for a "ghostbuster."

But the husband's pleas over the telephone had touched my heart. "Brad, please, I'm down on my luck. I lost my executive position in Chicago during the company's budget sweep two years ago. We took a terrible beating when we were forced to sell our home to pay major bills. We considered it a godsend when I was able to get a job here in this much smaller city and we were able to get this house at an extremely reasonable price. Now I'm beginning to see why we got such a bargain."

He (we'll call him George) went on to say that although he had always considered himself a good Lutheran who didn't believe in such things as ghosts and earthbound spirits, something that he could neither explain nor understand had made their life miserable almost immediately after they had moved into the old house.

"Anna and I have three kids, and they're scared to death of the weird things that happen. I'm afraid that Anna is on the verge of a nervous breakdown. The whole family keeps insisting that we move out of here immediately. But, man, I can not afford to move. I'm flat on my back financially. I need time to rebuild. Please come see what you can do to help us."

His words had moved me, but as I pulled into the driveway in front of the troubled Victorian mansion, I asked myself if I was truly the proper deliverer from whatever troublesome and restless spirits dwelt within the shadowed hallways and darkened rooms.

And now after I had heard each member's recitations of bizarre personal encounters with the "spooks," Anna was telling me with firm resoluteness that the center of the haunting lay in the attic.

"Terrible sounds of weeping come from there late at night," she said.

Had anyone ever investigated?

"No way!" George exclaimed, nearly spilling his cup of coffee over his lap. "There is no way in h…, ah, heaven that I would go up there when those crying noises begin."

Each of the three children echoed their father's sentiments with a "me neither" of their own.

Carol, fourteen, the oldest, had refused to stay alone in her room ever since the night something shook her bed and pulled her hair.

Mike, ten, swore that once when he was watching television, the set turned itself off, then back on, and "an ugly monster face" glared out at him from the screen.

Lewis, seven, spoke with unwavering conviction of the ghost kitty that kept appearing and disappearing and scattering his toys.

George had mainly been upset by the voices he had heard throughout the house. Apparently the haunting phenomenon was an excellent mimic, and he had been led on numerous "wild goose chases" when he was certain that he had heard members of the family calling him to the basement or to other rooms in the house. He had also heard the sounds of footsteps running throughout the entire home.

Anna had often found her clothes closet in a total disarray. Numerous personal items had completely disappeared.

And, of course, everyone had heard the sound of weeping issuing from the attic.

"It's so damned eerie," George shuddered involuntarily. "Just when it's finally quiet late at night, that damned crying starts in the attic."

Did it sound like a man or a woman crying?

George: "A woman."

Mike: "A little kid, maybe a girl, like seven or eight."

Lewis: "An old man, I think."

Carol: "I can't always tell. A man, though, I think."

Anna: "A man. Without question. A man who is very sad and disappointed about something awful that happened to him. Something he cannot bear to even think about. So he cries."

"Do you think maybe that someone got murdered in this house?" Carol asked.

"I'll bet they did!" Mike was certain. "You just know someone got murdered here."

"And the ghost could be out for revenge," Carol said, unable to suppress a shiver.

"And it'll take it out on us!" Mike shouted. "It's gonna kill us, Dad! We've got to move now…right now…tonight!"

Lewis started to cry in fear. He ran to his mother and buried his head in her lap. "Don't let the ghost kill us, Mommy!"

After a few moments of shouts, tears, and screams, George managed to restore order in his home.

"This is what it's been like, Brad," he said, his eyes pleading with me. "Please do something."

I asked to be left alone for a while. I needed time to center myself and to focus on what was taking place in the old house and what was so disturbing this family.

I had sat quietly for perhaps eight to ten minutes. I had been sitting with my eyes closed, but I opened them at the sound of the rustle of layers of clothing moving nearby. I could see nothing, but I felt a cool breeze against my face.

And then there were the whispers. Men's voices. Women's voices. At least two different children. Barely audible, jumbled phrases, perhaps a distinct word here and there, but generally blurred, slurred.

I heard the crying a few minutes later. It sounded as though it came from a source very far away, yet I knew that it issued from the attic.

Another sound nearer to me caused me to glance over my left shoulder. The entire family was wedged into a doorway, their eyes wide with fear, watching me to see what I was going to do.

One of my very favorite motion pictures with a paranormal theme is *The Uninvited* with Ray Milland, Ruth Hussey, and Gail Russell. I never fail to get a chill when the eerie specter of the woman begins to weep on the spiral staircase at night. I got a similar chill along my backbone at that moment, hearing those sobs of anguish coming from the attic. Only this wasn't a movie. This was real. And I was there.

But I had come to try to help this family.

"I'm going up to the attic," I said. "George, will you come with me?"

"No way!" he shouted, shaking his head vigorously in the negative. "I've been sleeping downstairs on the sofa for three weeks. There's no way I'll go upstairs after dark."

"I'll go with you," Anna said, moving away from the huddled mass of her family.

We were at the top of the stairs facing the narrow flight of steps that led to the attic when Anna suddenly pulled me into a storage room and motioned for me to keep quiet.

"I know what we'll find up there when we open the door to the attic," she said in a hoarse whisper.

The sounds of weeping were more distinct now that we stood nearer to the source. I could hear that they were definitely masculine in tone.

But Anna's behavior had me very puzzled. "If you know, why didn't you say something before?" I asked.

Her eyes filled with tears. "Because the awful thing that is in there is my terrible shame "

"You have something to do with what is in the attic?"

She nodded her head as she sought to compose herself.

The weeping had ceased, as if whatever was in the attic was waiting along with me for Anna to explain herself.

In the same hoarse whisper she told me her story:

"Ten years ago, I entered a big Chicago hospital to undergo an extremely serious surgery. I know that the doctors expected that I might die.

"After the surgery was completed, a new orderly wheeled me to what he thought was a recovery room. In actuality, it was a room near the morgue where half-a-dozen John Doe corpses from a terrible accident had been placed to await identification.

"When I opened my eyes, just awakening from the anesthesia, I had no idea where I was. I could just dimly see all these 'patients' lying near me on gurneys. The light in the room was quite dim; but when I could see better, I could distinguish all these corpses with gaping wounds lying all around me. I thought that I, too, must be dead.

"Since the hospital was a very large one, it was hours and hours before a nurse and an intern located me. I was nearly mad from the aftereffects of my surgery and my time among the corpses."

Anna emphasized that she had had a fear of death ever since she had been a child. Her ordeal at the hospital had accentuated her morbid fear to the farthest boundaries.

And then just a month before they had moved to this creaky old Victorian mansion, her father had died.

Anna's family was still very much Old World in many of their traditions. At her father's funeral, Anna's mother had bade her to kiss him goodbye before the casket was closed.

"I couldn't do it," she confessed, tears streaming over her cheeks. "My own father. I couldn't kiss him goodbye. My mother and my sisters got really upset with me, but I couldn't help it. I couldn't do it. I just couldn't bear to place my lips on Papa's cold flesh. I just couldn't do it."

I was sympathetic to Anna's difficult situation, but I was still puzzled as to the connection between the ghostly weeping emanating from the attic and her inability to kiss her father goodbye in his casket.

As if reading my thoughts, Anna glanced up at me, then bowed her head. "What is in the attic is my awful shame at not being able to kiss Papa goodbye. It is Papa who cries every night. He cries because Anna, his firstborn child, did not love him enough to kiss him goodbye as he lay in his casket."

Many years ago I wrote a book entitled, *Real Ghosts, Restless Spirits and Haunted Minds,* in which I hoped to demonstrate that energies that might have long lain dormant in a house could be activated by the "haunted mind" of a new resident. As I placed a consoling arm around Anna's shoulders, I recognized that whatever vibrations of past inhabitants had existed in the old Victorian mansion had been supercharged by that most haunting energy of all—guilt.

Just before we opened the door to the attic, we heard a whispered babble of voices. It was as if a theater audience sat within, awaiting the raising of the curtain on the evening's performance. Poor Anna kept her eyes closed tight, fully expecting to see her sorrowing Papa at stage center, awaiting her penance.

When we opened the door, the voices ceased so quickly it felt as if we had somehow entered a vacuum.

I saw nothing, and I heard no other sound than Anna's sobs of relief.

Before I left that night, I spent quite a bit of time trying my best to explain to Anna that her father had now risen to a higher state of consciousness wherein a neglected kiss would mean nothing to him. He had graduated to a plane of higher awareness wherein unconditional love pulsated as the very heartbeat of all entities existing there. Family traditions were a product of earthly constructs that once may have had meaning in the physical reality, but he had now progressed to a nonphysical dimension where the only ties that bound were structured of pure love.

Next I counseled the entire family on how best to go on with their lives without permitting fear constructs to distort their rational thought processes. I explained that they had inadvertently stirred up a psychic hornets' nest and that they would now have to remain as calm, cool, and collected as possible to give those buzzing energies a chance to expend themselves. Unless for whatever reasons the family chose to keep the energies active, the "ghosts" would soon re-enter another period of dormancy and completely leave them alone.

Although I knew that money was tight for them at the present time, I suggested that they enter into a family project of remodeling the house a little at a time. I had once done this to a "haunted" home of my own. I recommended that they repaint all the walls, replace the old plumbing, the old window frames, and every single one of the electrical fixtures. At the same time, they might want to replace all the previous wiring.

As best I could, I explained that ghosts may be manifestations of past events that have been brought to the minds of people sensitive enough to receive a kind of "echo" from the past. Emotion-charged events may somehow leave a trace vibration in the inanimate objects at the place where they occurred. This information, this memory may be transmitted telepathically to some deep level of the human unconscious; so if we remove as many artifacts of the past from a location, we may also be eliminating those impressions that can manifest in the conscious mind as "ghosts."

About two weeks later, I received a thank-you note from George and Anna in which they said that things had quieted down enough to allow for the "regular functions of normal family living—if, indeed, one might ever term our family as 'normal.' "

Since I never heard from them again, I assumed that Anna came to peace with her self-perpetuated guilt and that the haunting phenomena that had been activated by her troubled mind was simply allowed to run its course and return to its cosmic cocoon.

I think frequently of this case, however, because it illustrates so well how the human psyche, the "attic," so to speak, of the physical body, can unleash frighening ghosts or hideous monsters of its own that can frighten the hardiest of individuals.

And so I ask in this introduction to a book of some of my favorite, true stories of ghostly and eerie paranormal happenings, "Is your attic haunted?"

In their book *Body, Memory and Architecture*, Kent Bloomer and Charles Moore theorize that each of us has a place in our bodies— likely somewhere in our abdomen—that feels like our physical center, and so it is with our houses. The first floor, Bloomer believes, has a level of comfort akin to the gut. If, however, we move one floor up or down, we are pursuing trouble or adventure.

The basement, rather than corresponding to our feet, represents the dark side of our nature. The basement is the place in the house closest to the earth, so it may as well be a grave or a home for demons.

The attic, 'way upstairs, represents the brain; and since it is the part of the house closest to heaven, it should be a storehouse for pleasant memories of the past.

If, however, those memories have become dark, dank, and distorted by grief, greed, envy, jealousy, or hate, then it has become a haunted place—and there is something awful in the attic!

—BRAD STEIGER
Forest City, IA

lady martha and the little girl who wasn't there

The voice at the other end of the telephone line seemed to be nervously sincere, but I could not refrain from asking what appeared to be an obvious question: "Do you mean that you are actually afraid of this...this ghost?"

The man to whom I was speaking had been a tough and hardened combat paratrooper in World War II, and he was still a man with whom one would not wish to trifle in a physical confrontation. He took a deep breath, then sighed and delivered what was probably an unconscious paraphrasing of Hamlet's admonition to Horatio:

"All I'm going to say, Brad, is that there are a lot of things between Heaven and Earth that we simply do not understand, and the ghost of Lady Martha is certainly one of them!"

"But," I pressured slightly, "you have actually decided against having Irene Hughes and me visit the site of the haunting because you fear retaliation from this ghost?"

"We don't want you to come," he said frankly and directly. "Especially after what happened with your friend's tape recorder. Goodbye."

1

I held the buzzing receiver in my hand for a few moments, then returned it to the cradle. I was very disappointed, and I regretted having to call Irene and tell her that what had sounded like a dandy haunting and a promising research trip had suddenly been canceled by the percipients' fear of revenge from a touchy ghost.

In modern times, as difficult to believe as it may be for the skeptical reader, sensible, well-educated, practical men and women still fear the supernatural, the unknown.

Sophisticated moviegoers may enjoy being cinematically frightened and titillated by horror films and afterward engage in bold laughter and self-conscious analysis of the manner in which they were able to temporarily suspend reality and enter into the frightening illusion brought about by the creators of the eerie motion picture. But take these same sophisticated individuals, place them in an environment of moss-covered crypts, moldering mansions, and mournful midnight sighs floating up circular stairwells, and some peculiar atavistic mechanism transforms them into shuddering, haunted men and women.

Take, for example, the hard-nosed businessman who had just hung up on me.

A good friend of mine had called some days previously to inform me that he had found a dramatic instance of what seemed to be a classical haunting in his home town. According to the information he had gathered, the ghost of a strong-willed woman was haunting an entire office complex. The woman, whom everyone respectfully had called "Lady Martha" in life, was, according to certain percipients, even more imposing in death.

Lady Martha had been the kind of woman, who, opposed to smoking, would walk up to a total stranger on the street, slap a cigarette out of his mouth, and deliver a blistering lecture on the evils of nicotine. If cigarettes aroused her ire, beer and liquor drove her into an absolute frenzy of rage. Those who had known Lady Martha and her opinions said that her oratory on temperance and the wonderfulness of prohibition made Carrie Nation and her hatchet seem an ineffectual protester.

Some time after Lady Martha's death, so the story was told to my friend, an executive in the office building which she had owned and in which she had maintained a top floor apartment shook a cigarette out of a pack on his desk. He hung the cigarette on his lower lip, reached for a match—but before he could light the tobacco, the cigarette and the pack on his desk had vanished.

A thorough search of the office could not turn up even one crumb of the executive's tobacco. Word began to spread that Lady Martha's "no smoking" rule still held firm in her office building, and what is more, the lady herself was somehow still around to enforce it.

A clothing store located in the same building had been undergoing a series of peculiar happenings which seemed to reach a bizarre kind of climax one night after work when certain of the sales personnel decided to have a few relaxing beers in a basement storeroom. Since the salesmen were married and the saleswomen were young coeds from the local college, a decision was made to bolt the fire door behind them so that someone would not happen upon their innocent after-work libation and misinterpret the scene to the men's wives.

As the beer was being distributed, one of the men jokingly commented that it was a good thing that Lady Martha was in her grave or she would be able to smell the booze in her basement.

According to all those in attendance on that occasion, the words had scarcely been uttered when the bolted door swung open with a violence that slammed it against the wall. Then, to their immediate astonishment and their subsequent fear, a shimmering replica of Lady Martha drifted into the storeroom and shook a scolding finger at each participant in the after-hours beer bust.

When my friend, who is also a businessman in that same city, began to hear repeated accounts of such confrontations with the unknown in Lady Martha's office building, he called me and asked if he might arrange for psychic Irene Hughes and myself to visit the scene of the manifestations. He knew that Mrs. Hughes and I were extremely interested in being present at psychically infected sites in order that we might test her ability to gain paranormal impressions of the origin of such phenomena.

I agreed with his assessment that he had uncovered a story with a most interesting investigative potential, and I asked him if he might tape record an interview with some of the percipients of the phenomena so that I might evaluate the material personally before I made arrangements for Irene Hughes and myself to travel to his city.

My friend earnestly complied with my request, but it was that simple act of tape recording that led to the businessman's fearful squelching of our visit to the haunted office building of Lady Martha.

At first the businessmen had no objections to their taking time to give my friend an interview regarding the phenomena which they had witnessed and they had no objections to my bringing Irene Hughes to the building for the express purpose of conducting a séance in that basement storeroom where Lady Martha's ghost had so dramatically and forcefully appeared. In fact, they remarked that they would be honored to have so well-known and so well-respected a lady as Irene Hughes as a guest in their city.

But then, as a courtesy, my friend offered to play back the tape so that they would be able to hear their comments before he mailed the cassette to me. Unexplainably, whenever any of them mentioned Lady Martha's name, the tape went blank, so that the tape was full of such lines as, "Yes, I remember the time that _____ stopped me in my office to lecture me about smoking. Boy, could _____ ever preach against man's enslavement to tobacco."

And that was that. The men blanched and looked warily about the room, as if expecting to see an angry, shimmering form manifesting itself in a darkened corner.

Before my friend left them that evening, the businessmen were no longer eager to have a psychic and a reporter of the strange and unusual visit their building. They had enough of the strange and unusual happening about them every day, thank you, and the little demonstration that evening had convinced them that Lady Martha did not wish to have any spook hunters prowling around her building.

More than one of the men expressed his concern that if things had been "funny" and "weird" up to then, think what it would be like if Lady Martha really got angry with them for bringing in outsiders.

"In other words, Brad," my friend explained over the telephone, "we have a situation in which a group of normally hard-nosed, tough-minded businessmen are actually afraid of a ghost. I'm sorry

I blew it," he apologized. "I never should have played back the tape for them."

I told my friend that he could hardly be held responsible for the strange malfunctioning of his tape recorder, which had either presented us with a most peculiar audio coincidence or had provided us with a record of a dramatic kind of ghostly interference with a mechanical device. I did, however, ask for the home telephone number of the businessman who had been most eager for us to visit the haunted office building. I hoped that I might be able to appeal to him to persuade the others to change their minds and allow us to enter their offices for purposes of psychical research.

Although he seemed reluctant to speak with me, the businessman did accept my call. He remained unimpressed by my arguments, however, and stated bluntly that even if we were to travel the distance to his city, none of the men would speak with us and none would provide us access to the building. My last desperate ploy of attempting to shame a combat-scarred veteran of World War II by expressing my incredulity at the possibility of his being afraid of a ghost had only succeeded in his bringing our conversation to a rather abrupt close.

I must confess that this initial abortive attempt at a psychic safari with Irene Hughes proved to be a very wide eye-opener for me. In my books and articles and personal appearances, I have spent a great many words attempting to demonstrate to skeptical reading, listening, and viewing audiences that such things as telepathy, mind-over-matter, ghosts, and prophecy do have a place in our world of reality. Now I had just had a representative of the conservative and practical world of business inform me that he did most certainly believe in a plane of existence beyond our own. In fact, he believed in it to the point of fear.

Our next attempt at a psychic safari proved to be much more successful. Irene received a letter from a woman in Wisconsin who feared for the health and safety of a close friend who was living in a haunted house.

Here, again, we had a classic case of a haunting that will surely sound as though it all had been devised by a writer of gothic romances.

First of all, the house harbored poltergeist phenomena. Everything from dolls to dishes might become instantly transformed into ghostly guided missiles that would often pelt the occupants of the house, but never seriously injure anyone. The teenage daughter would frequently find her room in disarray when she returned home from school, and she noted that this bit of mischief would occur most often after a morning when she had taken careful pains to straighten up her room before leaving home. On the other hand, if she were to leave her room in a mess, she would often find that some invisible "brownies" had set the bedroom in order for her—right down to the last curler and comb.

The phenomena seemed to be centered in the attic, and the family reported that they often heard the sounds of something heavy being dragged across the floor. Although the house was quite large, the entire family circle, which was composed of father, mother and three children, aged nineteen to six, slept in two rooms downstairs. No one slept upstairs. On occasion, the mother told us, the teen-aged daughter would adamantly announce that she was not to be driven from her room and she would often sleep alone upstairs for as long as two to three weeks. Then the sound of mumbled half-words about her ears and the stroking of invisible fingers against her cheeks and hair would at last drive her back downstairs to join the rest of the family in the relative quiet of the two back bedrooms.

The other center of the haunting was located in the basement. The phenomena in the eerie area under the house consisted primarily of knockings, thumpings, and the sound of footsteps running down the stairs and shuffling across the floor.

The most dramatic manifestation of the haunting was realized in the materialization of four skeletons, which, after appearing in startling blood-red color, would slowly clothe themselves in the flesh of a man, two women, and a young girl. Each of the images appeared in period dress of about the late 1900s.

While the members of the Wisconsin family watched in horror, a bizarre ethereal tableau unfolded before them. As the lovely, long-haired blonde girl sat idly playing with her dolls, the man in the ghostly drama strangled one of the women, while the other stood by with a pleased expression of immense satisfaction. To all superficial assessments, it appeared as though the haunting might very well have been set into motion by a tragic playing out of the eternal triangle. At one time, so the eerie paranormal production number seemed to be telling its percipients, the man of the house had either strangled his wife, or his mistress, to please the other.

This time we received eager confirmation from the lady of the psychically infected house. She was not about to forbid our driving up to the small Wisconsin lumber town. In fact, she all but begged us to make the trip.

We had not been in the home but a few minutes when I began to feel rather nauseated and decidedly uncomfortable. I had heard and read other investigator's reports of being similarly affected by certain haunted sites, but I had never been so afflicted in several years of prowling about allegedly haunted premises. After all, my parental home had provided the family with a continuing phenomena of treading footsteps and opening and closing doors, so I had always felt quite at home in other houses with similar manifestations. But now I could no longer ignore that which was making me increasingly aware of one of the unavoidable requirements of the human condition: I needed to find a bathroom.

To cover my embarrassment, I suggested that while Irene and others of our party conduct a preliminary interview with the lady of the house, I should scout around a bit and see if I might not discover a "cold spot" of the haunting. After all, I pointed out, my tape recorder was running right at the lady's elbow, and the others were perfectly capable of opening the interview.

Interestingly enough, I did run into an obvious cold spot in the house as I searched for a bathroom, but its significance soon diminished in comparison with a subsequent development.

While I was in the bathroom, I could clearly hear the sound of what was ostensibly the youngest girl playing with her dolls. She was singing a kind of semi-tuneless little song, the kind of mumbled, melodic chant that seems to be universal with children, especially little girls, at play. From time to time, she would interrupt her humming song to call rather loudly for her mother. Then, when there was no response, she would return to her playing and her singing.

As a father of two girls, I created a mental image of a little girl dressing her dolls, combing their hair, creating her own world of imagination with the aid of a semi-trance state partially induced by her play-time chant. I determined that the sound was coming from upstairs, almost directly above me. (I had yet to learn that no member of the family, with the exception of that stubborn teenage daughter, ever went upstairs alone.)

When I rejoined the group, my discomfort had passed and I was prepared once again to assume the role of a bold and fearless ghost hunter. I excused myself for interrupting the conversation in progress, announced that I had found a cold spot, then, with additional apologies for asking what may have been an already asked question, I inquired of the woman just how many children she had.

She replied that she had three: a son in his late teens, who did not always live at home with them; a teenage daughter in high school; and a six-year-old girl, the only child whom she had had by her second and present husband.

"May we meet the children?" I wished to know.

"Oh," she apologized. "I sent them all over to friends' homes. I thought that that you would rather work without the interruption of children."

Irene told her that that was fine, that the investigation undoubtedly would proceed much smoother without the presence of the children.

I was puzzled by logic that would dictate that she saw to it that the older children were removed from underfoot, but retain the youngest child in the home, the child who would be most liable to pop up where she was not wanted. So I said:

"I suppose the little girl will just stay upstairs and play with her dolls?"

The woman blanched slightly and shifted uneasily in her chair. "My little girl is also at a friend's house."

I laughed, a bit louder than was necessary. "Then you'd better go upstairs and have a chat with her. She has come home to the company of her dolls."

"Up-upstairs?" the woman echoed. Her hand clasped her friend's arm for support. "You heard a little girl upstairs?"

I am not as dense as it may be beginning to appear to the astute reader. I was by now quite aware that this was one family who had a great deal of difficulty with their upstairs and that the woman sincerely believed her daughter to be at a friend's home. It was also obvious that the combination of these two factors had unnerved the woman. But my ears had heard too clearly the sounds of a little girl's song, of a little girl's calls to her mother, of a little girl's play noises for me to be convinced for even one moment that I had heard anything out of the ordinary, anything supernatural.

"Your little girl is upstairs," I said firmly, determined not to encourage any display of hysteria that might psychically feed whatever other ethereal organisms inhabited the house. "I heard her playing and singing."

"My little girl could...could not be upstairs," the woman answered softly. It was obvious that she was struggling to maintain control of her fear, trying not to permit her dread of the unknown to warp the sound of her voice. "She is afraid to go upstairs alone. Upstairs is where..."

She seemed unable to complete her sentence and her trembling hands brought a coffee cup to her lips.

"Upstairs is where the most things happen in this house," her friend said, taking up the thread of the statement. "About the little girl. Did you hear it calling for its mother?"

"Yes," I acknowledged. "From time to time, she would pause in her play and call for mother."

"She and her husband," the friend went on, "often wake up at night or in the morning hearing that little girl calling for its mother. Whenever they check the kids, they find them all sound asleep."

It took a personal exploration of the upstairs, the attic, the basement, and the yard to convince me that no little girl was playing somewhere in that home. If I truly heard what I believe that I heard in that Wisconsin home, then I either heard the sound of some lost and confused spirit-child, eternally calling for its mother, or I heard some ethereal kind of phonograph record, eternally reproducing the sounds of a former resident of that house whenever someone of the proper receptivity entered the environment.

However I might theorize about the haunting from the safety of distance, the manifestations constituted a persistent living nightmare for the occupants of the home. The woman appeared to be suffering psychic battle fatigue from her constant confrontation with the paranormal incidents in her home, and she would not walk in any area of the house other than the kitchen and the living room without someone at her side.

We explored the basement, wherein she had so often heard heavy footsteps, thuddings, and scrapings.

We ventured up to the attic wherein the family had so often heard the sound of heavy objects being dragged across the dusty floor. As we opened the door, we caught sight of a wispy something retreating to a darkened corner of the cluttered storage area. (Had we seen a ghost, an ectoplasmic spirit, or a floating bit of cobweb reflecting the sunlight?)

We visited each of the upstairs rooms and discovered two additional "cold spots."

Irene offered many psychic impressions as we walked from room to room. The woman gave immediate feedback to the psychic's comments, and in nearly all cases, she credited the seeress with correct "hits."

Suffice it to say that the case turned out to be even more complex than we had anticipated. There seemed to be factors working within the mother's own psyche that were psychically feeding the phenomena, and while there was no immediate exorcism of spirit or entity and no instant erasure of memory pattern, I do think that Irene Hughes' counseling session with the woman did prove to be of great value to the beleaguered housewife. Since our visit, according to available reports, the woman has been better able to ride out the psychic storm that swirls throughout her household, and her continued correspondence with Mrs. Hughes enabled her to deal with the forces that possess her home.

I generally favor the theory that a ghost is much more like an animated memory pattern than an entity of independent intelligence.

Once some as yet unidentified set of circumstances impresses a memory pattern upon a certain environment, the pattern, like a brief strip of film being fed into a projector whenever the proper conditions are fueled, keeps "remembering" the same bit of action day after day. It seems to me that the ghost-actor is as indifferent to the percipients who observe its regular performances as an actor on celluloid is to the audience in a theater. In my opinion, it would be as out of character for a ghost to take notice of a percipient and to engage that percipient in conversation as it would be for an image on a strip of film to suddenly step off the screen and begin to speak and interact with moviegoers in the front rows.

Now this is what a *ghost* is to me, and when I speak of ghosts, I am not referring to spirits or souls. I am not, in fact, making reference to survival beyond the death experience at all.

In my definition, a ghost is not an earthbound spirit condemned to wander a certain environment until it finds peace; it is rather a bit of ethereal drama that is for some unknown reason fixed in an atmosphere that has somehow trapped it in a pattern of reruns that may last for centuries until the energy is dissipated.

Throughout man's recorded history and as contemporary as the morning newspaper, sober and respectable men and women have published accounts of their confrontations with ghosts. Innumerable people have witnessed ghostly phenomena, but only a few of the more courageous and unorthodox have had the bravery to study them and to begin to scrub away the stain of superstition that has clouded ghosts for so long. It is now becoming possible to admit that one believes in such phenomena without suffering the slings and arrows of outraged scientists. Indeed, it would seem that those dogmatic scientists, who, when asked to assess a mass of raw data supplied by sober and reliable witnesses, openly scoff at such material and refuse to examine it with grumblings that such things simply cannot be, are the ones who should bear the stain of the unenlightened. Such closed-minded and narrow individuals have been left far behind in the dusty ranks, as the army of knowledge advances on entrenched ignorance and superstition.

The question, then, is not whether people see ghosts. There is sufficient evidence to convince anyone who has managed to pry open a previously closed mind the least little bit that people really do see ghosts. Psychical research societies and independent investigators have files that bulge with accounts of men and women who have seen, heard, smelled, even felt ghosts.

The question is: What is it that these men and women have experienced? What *is* a ghost?

I have given my opinion that even though ghosts may appear to be as solid and material as a living being, there can be no verbal or physical interaction between ghost and percipient, because it is only the image of the ghost that is there, not its spirit.

A ghost represents a once-living human being in the same manner that a photograph represents him. Both are images of that person that have been in some way impressed upon certain artifacts in the environment.

But I must not be dogmatic with my theory. Dogma may well be the blight of learning and the curse of religion. It has always seemed to me that when one hears a learned gentleman insisting that something is so because someone *says* it is so, one can be reasonably certain that there remains a great deal of doubt about the matter under discussion. All of us, including our scientific High Priests, really know very little for certain about anything.

I shall probably do better by my readers if I readily concede that a ghost may be more than one kind of thing. A house may be haunted by the aforementioned concept of an animated memory pattern, but it may also be disturbed by things that are entities in their own right. In some cases, ghosts may be the spirits of those who left the earthly plane and found themselves irritated or discomforted by a task or lesson left undone. Ghosts may be symbols or memory pictures projected by the percipient's own mind. Or they may be entities from some other world or dimension—strange night creatures that somehow cross from one plane of reality to another.

I am an anomaly-seeking journalist, a phenomenologist, rather than a parapsychologist; but I am also the kind of reporter who cannot resist theorizing about the shadowy world that I love to explore. While I may favor the theory that most ghostly manifestations are the result of a memory pattern that has left a psychic residue powerful enough to make itself known to sensitive individuals when certain stimuli are present in the environment, I certainly will not deny that the spiritistic hypothesis may be totally applicable in many instances.

And what about the UFOs we shall encounter in this book? Well, the ones that we are going to investigate may be closer to "ghosts" in their actual composition and ultimate purpose than many researchers may realize at the present stage of our pursuit of the elusive objects. While it seems to me that no thinking person can deny the possibility of extraterrestrial intelligence somewhere in the limitless cosmos, so much of what we currently tend to classify as UFOs seem to behave more like ghostly phenomena than intergalactic visitors.

I freely admit that I am much more concerned with the philosophical and the spiritual implications of these kind of phenomena than I am with proving anything to the scientific satisfaction of anybody. I realize that in our twentieth century world of materialism and ever-expanding technology the academic parapsychologists feel compelled to prove the validity of psychical phenomena, and I understand why this must be so in order to gain credibility and the respect of their more orthodox scientific colleagues. But those who attempt to trap generally elusive psychic occurrences into laboratory test tubes in order to satisfy the scientific requirement of controlled and repeatable experiments have different roles to play than I do as an investigative reporter and communicator.

I feel it should be pointed out, however, that there are several phenomena under the aegis of orthodox science that do not lend themselves to the rigid demand for experimental replication. There is the whole area of natural phenomena, which must be observed at the moment of occurrence and cannot be controlled by any laboratory technician. Meteors, eclipses, lightning flashes, and the Northern Lights, for example, are transitory, sporadic phenomena incapable of being reproduced at the will of an investigating scientist; yet it would seem foolish should someone insist that they not be recognized by orthodox science.

To be frank, I rather doubt if the parapsychologists shall ever be able to offer their skeptical colleagues the kind of proof that is obtainable in such material sciences as chemistry and physics. I have heard it said that proof is an idol before which pure mathematicians torture themselves. Physicists seem generally satisfied to sacrifice themselves before the more accessible shrine of plausibility. It would seem to me that the best the psychical researchers can offer by way of proof would more nearly resemble the kind that is acceptable in a court of law. In other words, they may present evidence in an open and objective manner so that any reasonable person who chooses to examine all the evidence will conclude that the cons balanced by the pros indicate the probability of the psychic thesis.

Throughout the course of this book, we are going to be holding court in a lot of bizarre and eerie places. I cannot promise you any final answers as to the exact makeup of a ghost, the true place of origin for UFOs, or any ultimate definitions of reality; but I can promise you that you will never be bored.

the haunting of beavor lodge

On the very first night that Sir William Richmond and his family occupied Beavor Lodge, all the members of the household were disturbed by strange noises in the lower part of the house. Thereafter, the nightly rattling of windows and the thudding of spectral footsteps would be considered the most minor of the weird nuisances.

Doors would open just before members of the household entered a room—as if an invisible butler had turned the handles. Mournful sounds of someone sighing and sobbing could be heard at all hours of the day or night, especially in a certain back bedroom and on the little staircase that led to it. A strange sound, as of someone stitching coarse material, was often heard; and nearly everyone had the uneasy feeling of being watched.

Beavor Lodge could not have looked less like a haunted house. Built in the late 1700s by Samuel Beavor, the house was a simple, rectangular two-story brick building. The main feature of the estate was the lovely garden which was bordered on one side by the Thames and on the other by a country lane. When the Richmonds moved into the house in 1871, they were completely unaware that they were about to share the quarters with any sort of psychic phenomena. They knew of nothing in the house's history to indicate the presence of sobbing and sighing spooks.

Shortly after they had moved into Beavor Lodge and had begun to be aware of the bizarre nocturnal activity peculiar to that house, Mrs. Richmond overheard two ladies talking while riding on an omnibus. "There's Mrs. Richmond, who's just moved into Beavor Lodge," said one lady to the other. "I wonder how long they'll last when they find out how haunted it is?"

The Richmonds were most unusual people. They soon grew to tolerate the sobs and the sighs, the obliging doors that opened at their approach, and the invisible footsteps that hurried about the house most of the evening. For over five years, Sir William and his brave household patiently endured in their residence on the borderlands of the unknown. And then, in October, 1875, a startling new development was added to the haunting at Beavor Lodge.

Mrs. Richmond was reading to three of her children in the dining room. She had rung for the parlor maid to take a letter to the post office and, when she heard a door open, extended the letter so that the maid might take it from her hand. As she glanced up from the book, she was surprised to see a short woman dressed in a gray, filmy garment standing before her and the children. The children's backs were tuned to the strange woman, so Mrs. Richmond said nothing that would frighten them. Instead, she continued reading without dropping a syllable, while at the same time keeping a surreptitious watch on the uninvited guest. At last the woman, through with her observation of the children, turned to leave the room. But before she had reached the door, she had disappeared as completely as if she had never been there.

Although Mrs. Richmond reported the incident to her husband and to no one else, the servants were soon seeing the apparition, too. One servant, who had been with the Richmonds at Beavor Lodge from the beginning and had long since grown accustomed to the house's peculiar moans and groans, gave her notice after she had confronted the apparition of the woman in gray on the staircase.

One night, Mrs. Richmond was awakened by screams of terror coming from her six-year-old daughter, who slept in a small room next to her parents. Sir William ran to his daughter's bedside and received her report that she had seen "a wicked-looking old gray woman, with a horrid face standing at the foot of the bed looking at me."

In the autumn of 1876, Mrs. Richmond had just fallen asleep when she was awakened by loud sobs in her room. An icy wind seemed to blow through her chamber as the curtains of her bed were pulled back, and an invisible hand reached in to pull her hair.

After this, she often heard a voice calling her name: "Clara! Clara!" Thinking that it was her husband, she would run to his study only to find him quite surprised by her charge that he had been calling her. Once, however, they nearly collided in a passageway. He had been coming to her because he claimed to have heard her voice calling his name.

Sir William remained singularly unimpressed with the haunting until he stayed alone at Beavor Lodge while his family was away in the country. Only one servant, a cook, remained behind. The master of Beavor Lodge set about enjoying the quiet of an empty household by spending his evenings in his study, catching up on his reading.

One night he had lit up his pipe, found his place in his book, scratched the ear of his collie dog, and began to read. There was ample light in the study; a reading lamp was positioned on a table next to Sir William's chair and a blazing fire crackled in the fireplace. He had become absorbed in his book when the collie pricked up its ears and gave a low, rumbling growl of warning.

Sir William frowned his impatience at the interruption as the handle of the door shook. When no one entered the room, Richmond sighed and muttered something about the cook not being able to make up her mind. The dog continued to growl and pressed up against its master's legs as if it were terrified.

A distinct feeling of unease pricked the back of Sir William's neck. Slowly he looked around. There, about twelve feet from his chair, stood the figure of a woman clothed in a long, flowing robe. He could not distinguish the specter's face, as it was shrouded in a veil that clung mistlike to her features. The phantom remained in Sir William's study for several moments while the collie whined in terror. Then, just as unexpectedly as it had come, the apparition vanished.

It was about this time that George Richmond, who was Sir William's celebrated artist-father, uncovered the legend behind the haunting of Beavor Lodge. According to the story that he had heard, counterfeiters had at one time taken up residence in the house; when they discovered a woman spying on them, they had sewn her up in a sack and tossed her unceremoniously into the Thames.

"That explains the terrible sounds in this house," George Richmond told his son. "The strange sound of sewing, the horrible sobs of a woman in terror of her life."

No sooner had the Richmonds accepted the phantom presence of the Gray Lady, who had been done away with the counterfeiters, than another sorrowing specter began to appear in their garden. This apparition, also a woman, took her spectral stand beneath a pear tree. The Society of Psychical Research had long since become interested in the strange doings at Beavor Lodge, and the famous investigators, Gurney and Myers, held a séance with a medium, Mrs. Augustus De Morgan, in an attempt to learn the identity of the mysterious lady in the garden.

According to Mrs. De Morgan, the sorrowing woman was a girl who belonged to a convent; she had become pregnant and had murdered the ensuing child to conceal her guilt. The body had been buried in that spot long before Beavor Lodge was built and the garden planted.

Richmond later wrote that Mrs. De Morgan was "an extremely sensible lady of exceptional accomplishments which, by their nature, were directly opposed to undue credulity. She was a good scholar, the daughter of a hard thinker, the wife of a great mathematician, deeply religious in her own way, and a great friend of Carlyle. A lady of strong, independent judgement, she quite satisfied herself of the truth of this story."

In later years, Mrs. De Morgan found a way to "communicate" with the shade of the Gray Lady who sobbed in the darkened corners of Beavor Lodge. According to the Richmonds, Mrs. De Morgan at last set the troubled spirit to rest, and nothing more was ever seen or heard of the phenomena that had disturbed domestic life at Beavor Lodge for over twenty-five years.

At the cessation of the disturbances, Sir William said: "Upon such matters as ghosts I confess I keep an open mind. I neither believe nor disbelieve in them, nor the possibilities of their reentry into a world which the body has left. That speculation must always be interesting upon such matters I acknowledge; but for myself I decline to study the question from a scientific standpoint because I believe that science is incapable of dealing with the Infinite…The Mysteries by which Matter and life are surrounded will never be solved by German Chemists."

the vicious devil
of borley

When the Reverend Mr. Brown opened the cabinet in the library to put away some books, he was startled see a human skull grinning at him from a shelf.

"I say, dear," he called to his wife after he had recovered from his shock, "come look at this."

Mrs. Brown sucked in her breath as her husband moved the skull from the cabinet and began to examine it. "You don't suppose," she asked with nervous laughter, "that the rectory really is haunted?"

Reverend Brown smiled. "More than likely the rector who preceded us here had an unusual taste in paperweights."

"You don't think that could be the skull of the nun that's supposed to walk through these halls," Mrs. Brown persisted, "or the skull of one of those poor devils who was buried in the Plague Pit?"

"Easy now," her husband cautioned, "or you'll have yourself believing all the weird tales we've heard about Borley Rectory."

"But you cannot deny the fact that no fewer than a dozen clergymen refused to live here before you accepted the call," Mrs.

21

Brown said. "Nor can you deny that a former rector had that window in the dining room bricked up because he could not stand to see the ghost of the nun continually peering in at him."

Reverend Brown tried to ignore his wife's suggestion that "something evil" had made its abode in the rectory. He and the sexton gave the skull a solemn burial in the churchyard, and he and his wife fought to stave off the depression that seemed to have enveloped them. It was not many nights, however, before they were given awesome evidence of invisible forces at work.

It usually began shortly after they had retired for the evening. They would be lying in bed, and they would hear the sound of heavy footsteps walking past their door. Mr. Brown soon took to crouching in the darkness outside of their room with a hockey stick gripped firmly in his hands. Several nights he lunged at "something" that passed their door—always without result.

Bells began to ring at all hours and became an intolerable nuisance. Hoarse, inaudible whispers sounded over their heads. Small pebbles appeared from nowhere to pelt them. A woman's voice began to moan from the center of an arch leading to the chapel. Keys popped from their locks and were found several feet from their doors. The Browns had found themselves living in what Dr. Harry Price would soon come to call "the most haunted house in England."

In the summer of 1929, Dr. Price answered the plea of the haunted rector and his wife. Leaving London, Dr. Price and an assistant drove to the small village of Borley, reviewing what they already knew about the eerie rectory. The building, though constructed in modern times, stood on the site of a medieval monastery whose gloomy old vaults still lay beneath it. Close at hand had been a nunnery, whose ruins were much in evidence. About a quarter of a mile away stood a castle where many tragic events had occurred, ending with a siege by Oliver Cromwell. There was a persistent legend about a nun who had been walled up alive in the nunnery for eloping with a lay brother who had been employed at the monastery. The lay brother, who received the punishment meted out for such sins, was hanged. Inhabitants of the rectory, and several villagers had reported seeing the veiled nun walking a path through the grounds. A headless nobleman and a black coach pursued by armed men had also been listed as a frequent phenomenon.

The present rectory had been built in 1865 by the Rev. Henry Martin. He had fathered fourteen children and had wanted a large rectory. He died in the Blue Room in 1892 and was succeeded in occupancy by his son, Lionel, who died at the rectory in 1927. The building was vacant for a few months—while a dozen clergymen refused to take up residence there because of the eerie tales which they had heard—until Reverend George Brown and his family accepted the call in 1928. The psychical researcher did not have to wait long for the phenomena to put on a show for him. Price and his assistant had just shared a lunch with Mr. and Mrs. Brown when a glass candlestick struck an iron stove near the investigator's head and splashed him with splinters. A mothball came tumbling down the stairwell, followed by a number of pebbles.

Price busied himself for the next several days with interviewing the surviving daughters of Henry Martin, the builder of the rectory, and as many former servants as had remained in the village. The eldest of the three surviving daughters told of seeing the nun appear at a lawn party on a sunny July afternoon. She had approached the phantom and tried to engage it in conversation, but it had disappeared as she had drawn near to it. The sisters swore that the entire family had often seen the nun and the phantom coach and that their brother, Lionel, had said that, when dead, he would attempt to manifest himself in the same way. It was their father, Henry Martin, who had bricked up the dining room window so that the family might eat in peace and not be disturbed by the spectral nun peeping in at them.

A man who had served as gardener for the Martin family told Price that every night for eight months he and his wife heard footsteps in their rooms over the stables. Several former maids or grooms testified that they had remained in the employ of the Martins for only one or two days before they were driven away by the strange occurrences which manifested themselves on the premises.

Mrs. Brown was not at all reluctant to admit that she, too, had seen the shadowy figure of a nun walking about the grounds of the rectory. On several occasions, she had hurried to confront the phantom, but it had always disappeared at the sound of her approach.

The Browns left the rectory shortly after Dr. Price's visit. They had both begun to suffer the ill-effects of the lack of sleep and the enormous mental strain which had been placed on each of them.

Borley Rectory presents an interesting combination of a "haunting" and the phenomenon of poltergeistic activity. Henry Price maintained that approximately one-half of all hauntings include some type of poltergeistic disturbance. There are those, of course, who will use such cases to "prove" their supposition that the poltergeist is truly a racketing ghost. Others will point out the possibility that whatever facet of mind is capable of producing the phenomena of the poltergeist may also be capable of activating the subconscious memory patterns of the dead that, in some way not yet known to science, have been impressed on the psychic ether. A child approaching puberty may be of just the proper telepathic affinity to allow these bottled-up memories to release their energy through the medium of his own fragmented psyche.

Henry Martin had fourteen children who lived in the rectory. Phenomena began to become active about ten years after he had moved into the rectory with his family. It is also interesting to record that the phenomena reached new heights of activity when the Rev. B. Morrison took up residence in the rectory on October 16, 1930. The Reverend brought with him his wife, Marianne, and his twelve-year-old daughter.

The Morrisons had lived there only a few days when Mrs. Morrison heard a voice softly calling, "Marianne, dear." The words were repeated many times, and, thinking her husband was summoning her, Mrs. Morrison ran upstairs. Mr. Morrison had not spoken a word, he told her, but he, too, had heard the calling voice.

Once, Mrs. Morrison laid her wristwatch by her side as she prepared to wash herself in the bathroom. When she completed her washing, she reached for the watch and discovered that the band had been removed. It was never returned.

Reverend Morrison was quick to realize that the weird tales that he had heard about Borley Rectory had all been true. He could hardly deny them in view of such dramatic evidence. He was not frightened, however, as he felt protected by his Christian faith. He used a holy relic to quiet the disturbances when they became particularly violent and remained calm enough to keep a detailed journal of the phenomena which he and his family witnessed.

Mrs. Marianne Morrison received the full fury of the poltergeist's attack from the very beginning of their occupancy. One night, while carrying a candle on the way to their bedroom, she received such a violent blow in the eye that it produced a cut and a black bruise which was visible for several days. A hammer-head was thrown at her one night as she prepared for bed. She received a blow from a piece of metal that was hurled down a flight of stairs. Another time, Mrs. Morrison narrowly missed being struck by a flat iron, which smashed the chimney of the lamp that she was carrying.

In addition to persecuting Mrs. Morrison, the poltergeist seemed determined to establish contact with her. Messages were found scrawled on the walls: "Marianne—please—get help."

The poltergeist may or may not have been suggesting that the Morrisons once again bring Dr. Harry Price upon the scene. At any rate, that is exactly what they did. Advised by the Martin sisters of the famed investigator's interest in the Borley phenomena, Reverend Morrison wrote to London to inform Dr. Price of renewed activity in the rectory.

Price gained permission to stay in the rectory with two friends and set out at once for the village. Upon arrival, the researcher and his party once again examined the house from attic to cellar. The phenomena wasted no time in welcoming the returning investigator. While he was examining an upstairs room, an empty wine bottle hurled itself through the air, narrowly missing him. The party was brought back down to the kitchen by the screams of their chauffeur, who had remained behind to enjoy a leisurely smoke. The distraught man insisted that he had seen a large, black hand crawl across the kitchen floor.

During conversation, Mrs. Morrison disclosed that she had seen the "monster" that had been causing all the eerie disturbances. Reverend Morrison showed Dr. Price the entry that he had made in his journal on March 28th when his wife had confronted the entity while ascending a staircase. She had described it as a monstrosity—black, ugly, ape-like. It had reached out and touched her on the shoulder with an "iron-like touch." Price later learned that others had seen the creature on different occasions.

The Morrisons also told Price and his team that the phenomenon had begun to produce items which they had never seen before. A small tin trunk had appeared in the kitchen when the family was eating supper. A powder box and a wedding ring materialized in the bathroom, and, after they had been put away in a drawer, the ring disappeared over night. Stone-throwing had become common, and Reverend Morrison complained of finding stones in their bed and under their pillows as well.

Although Reverend Morrison was a brave man, he had never enjoyed good health nor the kind of stamina necessary to outlast a poltergeist. It is, of course, a tribute to the family to record that they did stick it out at the rectory for five years before leaving in October of 1935. After the Morrisons had raised the white flag of surrender to the phenomena, the Bishop wisely decreed that the place was put up for sale, and it should have come as no surprise to the parish to discover that there would be no interested parties waiting in line to bid on it.

In May of 1937, Harry Price learned that the rectory was empty and offered to rent the place as a type of "ghost" laboratory. His sum was accepted, and the investigator enlisted a crew of forty men who would take turns living in the rectory for a period of one year. Price outfitted the place and issued a booklet which told his army of researchers how to correctly observe and record any phenomena which might manifest itself.

Shortly after the investigators began to arrive, strange pencil-like writings began to appear on the walls. Each time a new marking was discovered, it would be carefully circled and dated. Two Oxford graduates reported seeing new writing form while they were busy ringing and dating another. It appeared that the entity missed Mrs. Morrison. "Marianne...Marianne...M..." it wrote over and over again. "Marianne...light...Mass...prayers"; "Get lights"; "Marianne...please...help...get."

The organized investigators were quick to discover a phenomenon which had not been noted by any of the rectors who had lived in Borley. This was the location of a "cold spot" in one of the upstairs passages. Certain people began to shiver and feel faint whenever they passed through it. Another "cold spot" was discovered on the landing outside of the Blue Room. Thermometers indicated the temperature of these areas to be fixed at about 48 degrees, regardless of what the temperature of the rest of the house may have been.

The "nun" was seen three times in one evening by one observer, but was not noticed at all by any of the other investigators. A strange old cloak kept the researchers baffled by continually appearing and disappearing. Several of Price's crew reported being touched by unseen hands.

On the last day of Dr. Price's tenancy, the wedding ring once again materialized. The investigator snatched it up, lest it disappear, and brought it home to London with him.

Professor C. E. M. Joad, of the Department of Philosophy and Psychology at the University of London was one of those who witnessed the pencil markings appearing on the walls. In the July, 1938 issue of *Harper's Magazine*, Professor Joad commented on this experience. "…having reflected long and carefully upon the squiggle I did not and do not see how it could have been made by normal means…. The hypothesis that poltergeister materialize lead pencils and fingers to use them seems to be totally incredible…. And the question of 'why' seems hardly less difficult to answer than the question 'how.' As so frequently occurs when one is investigating so-called abnormal phenomena, one finds it equally impossible to withhold credence from the facts or to credit any possible explanation of the facts. Either the facts did not occur, or if they did, the universe in some respects be totally other than what one is accustomed to suppose."

In late 1939, the Borley Rectory was purchased by a Captain W. H. Gregson, who renamed it "The Priory." He was not at all disturbed by warnings that the place was haunted, but he was upset when his faithful old dog went wild with terror on the day they moved in and ran away never to be seen again. He was also mildly concerned with the strange track of unidentified footprints that circled the house in fresh fallen snow. They were not caused by any known animal, the captain swore, nor had any man made them. He followed the tracks for a time until they mysteriously disappeared into nothingness.

Captain Gregson did not have long to puzzle out the enigma of Borley. At midnight of January 27, 1939, the "most haunted house in England" was completely gutted by flames. Captain Gregson testified later that a number of books had flown from their places on the shelves and knocked over a lamp, which had immediately exploded into flame.

the awful room
at willington mill

For two months the nursemaid had tried to ignore the strange
noises that she had heard coming from the deserted room over
the nursery. The sounds came each night when she was left alone
to watch the child—a dull, heavy tread, like someone slowly pacing back and forth.

For eight weeks she had chosen to ignore the sounds, but now, she
announced to her employer, Mr. Joseph Proctor, she was asking to be
discharged from his service. "I am persuaded that it is something supernatural up there, and it has quite upset me," she told him.

As the woman was obviously in a state of great nervous agita-
tion, Proctor saw no reason why he should attempt to talk her into
staying with them. It wasn't long, however, before he too heard the
sound of heavy feet in the upstairs room, as did his wife and the
other servants. Although puzzled by the eerie tread of invisible feet,
the Proctors convinced themselves that there was undoubtedly some
natural explanation for the phenomenon.

In spite of their refusal to take the noises seriously, they purposely omitted any mention of the disturbed room when they hired

a new nursemaid on January 23, 1835. On her first evening in the nursery, the girl came down to the sitting room to inquire who was in the room above her. The Proctors evaded her questions, putting the whole matter down to "just the usual night noises in an old house."

The next day, Mrs. Proctor heard the steps of a man with heavy boots walking about in the upstairs room. That same day, while the family was at dinner, the nursemaid came down the stairs and blinked incredulously at Mr. Proctor. "I've been hearing someone walking in the room above me for five minutes," she told him. "I had come down to assure myself that it wasn't you, sir. But if it isn't you, who is it?"

Proctor inspected the room that night. Trickery seemed out of the question. The empty room was covered with a thin, undisturbed layer of soot, which in itself was proof that not even a mouse had been walking about on the floor. The window had been boarded up many years ago with wooden laths and plaster, and the door to the room had been nailed shut for some time. Proctor descended even more mystified then when he had gone up to conduct his investigation.

On the 31st, the Proctors heard a dozen loud thuds sound next to their bed as they were preparing to retire. On the next night, Joseph Proctor heard a metallic rapping on the baby's crib: There was a brief pacing overhead, and then the sound of footsteps, which were never heard again in the upper room.

But what followed for the next several years included such visible and auditory manifestations that the plodding footsteps were to seem like a baby's first steps in comparison. What is nearly as remarkable as the intense "haunting" of Willington Mill is the fact that the Proctors persisted in living in the house for over eleven years before finally surrendering to some of the most eerie paranormal disturbances on record.

Thomas Mann, the foreman of the mill that was separated from the Proctor's house by a road and a garden, told Proctor that he had heard a peculiar noise moving across the lawn in the darkness. At first, Mann thought it came from the wooden cistern that stood in the mill yard, and he suspected that some pranksters were making off with it. Upon pursuing the noise with a lantern in hand, Mann had found nothing; and the cistern, he later testified, had not been budged. Mann also told Proctor in the strictest confidence that he had been hearing a sound like invisible steps on the gravel walk.

It was shortly after their confidential conversation that both Mann and another neighbor observed the luminous phantasm of a woman in a window of Proctor's house. Both parties had seen the apparition independent of each other, and Mann had called his entire family to witness the phantasm, which was fully visible for over ten minutes.

About a year after the phenomena were in full swing, Jane Carr, Mrs. Proctor's sister, arrived for a stay at the mill. A few minutes before midnight, she was awakened by a noise very much like that of someone winding a large clock. After this "signal noise," her bed began to shake and she clearly heard a sound like that of a heavy sack falling on the floor above. Several strong knocks sounded about her bedstead, and the unmistakable shuffle of feet surrounded her bed.

One night, the phenomena specialized in bed-lifting. It manifested itself under the older child's crib (the disturbances had not prevented the Proctors from producing a family) by raising the mattress until he cried out, then it hoisted the mattress of the bed on which Mrs. Proctor and a new nursemaid were sleeping. Mrs. Proctor described the sensation as feeling "as if a man were underneath pushing it up with his back."

In addition to feet, the poltergeist had soon acquired invisible hands with which to pound on walls and lift beds. These achievements would seem as child's play, however, as the thing began to develop its ability to whistle and talk and materialize itself into a number of grotesque phantoms.

The boys, Joseph and Henry, were awakened one night by a loud shriek, which had sounded from under their cribs. Joseph, Sr., upon investigating, heard an eerie moan coming from somewhere in the room. A bed began to move and the voice spoke its first words— or what sounded like the words, "chuck-chuck." These sounds were followed by a noise similar to that of a child sucking at a bottle. The youngest child, Jane, was moved to another room, but she was not spared the torment of having her bed levitated.

The phenomena had begun to leave its domain on the upper floor and go on foraging expeditions during the night. As is so often the case in poltergeist phenomena, the kitchen seemed to be a favorite target for its nightly forays. The cook would, on several mornings, find the kitchen chairs heaped in a disorderly pile, the shutters thrown open, and utensils scattered about the room.

Mrs. Proctor's brother, Jonathan Carr, spent a night filled with bed-shakings and whistlings and declared that he would not live in the house for any amount of money.

Jane Carr, Mrs. Proctor's sister, was much more strong nerved than her brother, and judging from Proctor's journal, the young woman spent many nights in the afflicted house. One night as she lay sleeping with the cook, Mary Young, the two women were terrified to hear the bolt in their door slide back, the handle turn, and the door open. Something rustled the curtains as it moved across the bed, then it lifted the bedclothes from the trembling figures. As it passed around the bed to Mary's side, both women distinctly saw a dark shadow against the curtain.

Little Jane Proctor was sleeping with her aunt Jane one night when she saw a strange head peeping out at her from the curtains at the foot of the bed. The four-year-old girl later described the head as being that of an old woman, but she became much too frightened to continue her observation and tucked her own head under the covers.

Joseph Jr. was disturbed nearly every night by some facet or other of the phenomena. He reported hearing the words, "Never mind" and "Come and get" being repeated over and over without any meaningful application. Footsteps were constantly parading around his bed, and thumpings sounded about his pillow and other bedclothes.

A Doctor Drury arrived and asked Proctor's permission to carry out an examination of the haunted upper room. Proctor consented and allowed the doctor and his companion, a young chemist, to make preparations to spend the night in the disturbed room. At about one o'clock in the morning, Proctor was awakened by a ghastly shriek of terror coming from the upper floor. Dr. Drury had come face to face with the spectre of the wizened old woman. The two "ghost hunters" spent the rest of the dark hours drinking coffee in the kitchen. They left the house at dawn. Proctor noted in his diary that the doctor had got "a shock that he will not soon cast off."

One of the most incredible materializations of the Willington Mill poltergeist was that of a monkey. Eight-year-old Joseph was seated atop a chest of drawers pretending that he was making a speech to the other children. Suddenly, in full view of all the children, including two-year-old Edmund (the third child that had been added to the family since the onset of the disturbances), a monkey appeared and began to tug at Joseph's shoe strap.

By the time Joseph, Sr., came running in response to their excited cries, the children were scurrying about the floor, trying desperately to play with the mischievous monkey. Two-year-old Edmund was looking under chairs until his bedtime, trying to locate the "funny cat."

Years later, the memory of that incident was still vivid in Edmund Proctor's mind. In the December, 1892 issue of the *Journal of the Society for Psychical Research*, he wrote: "Now it so happens that this monkey is the first incident in the lugubrious hauntings, or whatever they may be termed, of which I have any recollection. I suppose it was, or might easily be, the first monkey that I had ever seen, which may explain my memory being so impressed that I have not forgotten it. A monkey, and, upstairs in the nursery, that is the business. My parents have told me that no monkey was known to be owned in the neighborhood, and that after diligent inquiry no organman or hurdy-gurdy boy, either with or without a monkey, had been seen anywhere about the place or neighborhood, either on that day or for a length of time...

I have an absolutely distinct recollection of that monkey, and of running to see where it went to as it hopped out of the room and into the adjoining Blue-room. We saw it go under the bed in that room, but it could not be traced or found anywhere afterwards. We hunted and ferretted about that room, and every corner of the house, but no monkey, or any trace of one, was more to be found."

The white face of what appeared to be an old woman was seen more and more often, but Joseph Jr. soon added an old man to the list of materializations. Aunt Jane Carr did not see the monkey, but she reported that she had heard the "sound of an animal leaping down off the easy chair."

Another astonishing bit of ultra-sophisticated materialization took place when the entity fashioned a double of Joseph, beneath his bed, but imagine his shock upon discovering his mirror-image hiding from him in the shadows. The boy was, at this time, about ten years old so his powers of observation must be given some credence. Besides, having grown up in a most extraordinary home, he was inured to the average run-of-the-mill haunting. Joseph, Jr., said that his spectral self-image, which was even dressed in a manner identical to his, walked back and forth between the window and the wardrobe before it gradually dematerialized.

Shortly after this dramatic episode, the Proctors decided that they had endured enough. Patient Quakers though they were, eleven years of living amidst incessant psychic disturbances had been enough for them. They had also become fearful of "an unhappy effect, if not a permanent injury on the minds of their children should they remain longer in such a plague-ridden dwelling."

Proctor obtained a residence at Camy, Villa, North Shields, and after assisting with the packing, sent the servants and the children on ahead. The last night Mr. and Mrs. Proctor spent alone in Willington Mill was perhaps the most frightening of all.

Throughout the night they lay and listened to "boxes apparently being dragged with heavy thuds down the now carpetless stairs, non-human footsteps stumped on the floors…and impossible furniture…dragged hither and thither by inscrutable agency; in short, a pantomimic or spiritualistic repetition of all the noises incident to a household flitting."

One dreadful thought kept running through the Proctor's minds: the ghosts were packing to move along with them!

It was with indescribable relief that the Proctors arrived at the new residence to find it completely free of the former taint that had blemished eleven years of their lives. Their residency in the new home was blissfully untroubled by knockings, whistlings, footsteps, and phantasms.

the ghost in the lane carried a pitchfork

You know, Brad," Angie McWane told me in May of 1971, nearly a year after our midwestern psychic safari, "I can still see that sparkling, shimmering, swirling *something* that formed before us on that spooky lane leading to the old Sumter house." She gave a tiny shudder of recollection, then went on: "Some nights I even awaken and imagine that I can see it forming right in my bedroom!"

The eerie sight certainly had been impressive, and I don't think any of us who witnessed it on that warm July evening will ever forget it. In Angie's words, we "can still see it," building up before us like a misty collection of errant moonbeams.

Had we seen a ghost?

I don't know, but whatever it was, we all saw it on two consecutive nights. On the first night our psychic safari arrived in Iowa City, and Glenn McWane, our host in that city and a friend of mine who would be accompanying us, suggested that we drive out to take a look at a house that he had lined up for Irene's psychic inspection. It was midnight by then, the witching hour and all, but I am certain that each of our crew was quite inured to such suggestions of the "high-dark" twelve being any more magical than the "high-noon" twelve.

Glenn was driving my station wagon and he edged it cautiously into the lane. "We can only drive in just far enough to get off the street," he explained.

We soon saw the reason why when the headlights picked up the image of a wooden gate bearing an inscription advising any trespassers to keep out or risk being prosecuted.

"I've arranged for the caretaker to be with us tomorrow," Glenn told us. "I've also asked a policeman to accompany us just to be certain a passing squad car doesn't pick us up as vandals."

"This looks like a jungle," Irene complained, referring to the heavy overgrowth of weeds and bushes and the thick, drooping branches of untrimmed trees that virtually blanketed the narrow lane. "Where's the house?"

"I don't think you will be able to see more than the edge of it through all these trees," Glenn said. "It's hard to believe that this was once one of Iowa City's loveliest estates. But time and vandals...."

"What's that?"

I don't remember who first saw it and cut off Glenn's explanation of how the ravages of time and disinterest had wiped away the old estate's beauty, but no one had to point out the sudden intruder upon the dark and quiet scene. It appeared, to me, to be a very large, glowing orb of wispy light.

"Turn out the headlights, Glenn," I said.

"Yeah," Glenn nodded, pushing in the light switch, reading my thoughts, "maybe they're reflecting off something."

The strange orb glowed as brightly in total darkness with the headlamps shut off. Whatever the thing was, it seemed to have an independent light source.

The moon was covered by clouds that night. The nearest street light was a vapor-light, completely cut off from the old estate by the thick wall of trees. Actually, it would have been difficult for a powerful searchlight to have penetrated the tangled greenery and heavy plant growth and reached the dark pocket in the lane where the eerie light was glowing.

"How far away is it?" someone asked from the back seat of the station wagon.

"I would say that it is in the lane opposite the front door of the house," Glenn replied. "And that's probably forty to fifty yards from where we are sitting right now."

Glenn turned the headlights back on, and it appeared, whether optical illusion or what, that the orb of light was moving toward the old house.

Everyone turned to look at Irene, who was seated in the middle of the backseat. In the dim glow of the dashboard lights, I noticed a rather strange expression on her face, and it had occurred to me that she had been extremely quiet during our excitement over sighting the weird light.

"Shall we go right now and investigate the…whatever it is?" someone wondered.

"No," Irene answered, breaking her silence. "Not tonight. I have a very bad feeling that it would not be good for us to walk down that lane right now." There was a certain tone to her voice that indicated that she meant exactly what she said. Her psychic impression told her that the time was not right to invade the darkened lane and approach the shimmering orb that seemed more and more to be drifting toward the deserted house.

"Let's leave…*now!*" Irene said suddenly.

No one argued with her.

It was nearly midnight again on the second night when we approached the eerie mansion that had been so recently violated by vandals and frequented by some nameless thing that had been witnessed by several neighbors, as well as a number of policemen.

"I got my lead on this house from some cops," Glenn had explained. "Before the house was vacated, two old sisters lived alone here. Nearly every night a glowing, ghost-like *something* would appear, and the sisters would sit calmly and converse with it. On several occasions, the police got calls from neighbors who had seen the thing. I don't know what these people thought the police should do about the spook-light, and I guess the police didn't know either. They would just sit in their squad cars outside the house and watch the two old ladies talking with the glowing ghost. After one of the sisters passed on and the other was taken to a nursing home, the ghostlight continued to make its appearance every now and then."

Earlier that day, in the company of the caretaker, we had walked around the house and allowed Irene to pick up psychic impressions about its past inhabitants. I'll present that material a bit later, but right now, I would like to relate details of our second spotting of the ghost in the lane.

On this night, we had the caretaker and a policeman with us in the station wagon. We opened the gate, drove cautiously down the lane. When we were adjacent to the old house, Glenn stopped the car.

"Let us just sit quietly for a few moments," Irene requested, "and permit me to gain some psychic impressions of the house by night."

As Irene sat in meditation, I glanced absently out the windshield. I blinked my eyes rapidly. I wanted to be certain that I was really seeing something before I nudged the policeman who was sitting next to me.

Unless I was badly mistaken, there seemed to be a slight tendril of mist-like substance forming directly in front of the station wagon's hood. Only a few more seconds of observation were necessary to convince me that my eyes were not playing tricks on me. I nudged the policeman.

"I see it," he said before I could whisper any comment to him.

"What is it?"

"Dunno," he replied honestly.

"I've been watching it for a couple of minutes now," Glenn whispered in response to our overheard conversation. "It seemed to come from that clump of bushes over there, then stop directly in front of the car."

By now everyone was watching the glowing, mist-like thing, and we all sat in silence for a few moments, as we watched the orb growing larger and denser.

Glenn turned the headlights back on, and we could see that the substance was palpable enough not to be dissipated by the powerful headlamps. Glenn shut the lights off again, and we decided to get out of the car for a closer inspection.

"Is it ectoplasm?"

"A will-o'-the-wisp?"

"Maybe it's just night fog."

The small group of people who had accompanied us offered their queries and conjectures, as we surrounded the swirling, glowing, mist-like thing.

It was a very warm evening, but as I extended my hand into the midst of the mist, I seemed to feel cold. Or was that only my imagination?

"Could it be just a puff of vapor squeezed out of the cooling ground?" I asked the policeman.

"But why isn't there more of it?" he answered with a question of his own. "I mean, there's that field over there, and it doesn't have any mist in it. Here's all these trees and bushes, and there isn't any mist among them. Why is it forming just in this spot right in front of the station wagon?"

But then the thing seemed to be weary of our conjectures and our examination, and it was suddenly gone.

Before we could speculate on this rapid disappearance, Irene whispered loudly from the other side of the station wagon: "There are some people coming through the bushes by the house!"

I did not hear the sounds of footsteps and crackling brush myself, but others in the group swore that they could hear the approach of two or more people coming toward us.

Then the footsteps stopped, and one of our group directed our attention to the reappearance of the glowing mist between two trees. But before anyone could approach it, the light winked out as rapidly as if it had been an extinguished candle flame.

I moved to Irene's side.

"I swear they looked real to me, more than spirit," she was saying to Glenn. "But, of course, spirit can sometimes appear just as real as...."

"Did you see anything, Glenn?" I asked my friend.

"A white, misty thing that moved," he told me. "Right over there." He stabbed the spot with the beam of his flashlight. "We had seen it before."

"We heard something wailing through leaves and pushing aside the bushes," Irene said. "When I looked over there, I saw the forms of people moving toward us."

"I could only see this glowing glob," Glenn said almost apologetically.

"Perhaps Irene's greater sensitivity enabled her to see images where you could only see this glowing mist," I offered.

Irene suddenly put her hands to her ears.

"What's wrong?" Glenn and I chorused in sharp whispers.

"I hear someone screaming, screaming just terribly! She's calling for help!" Irene replied. "Oh," she said, feeling the pain in a momentary jab, "she's broken her leg."

"There! There in the bushes." Irene directed us. "See her head?"

"I see some of that glowing mist again," I told her.

"Yes," Irene agreed, "but look. I can see her very clearly."

"I see a clump of mist," Glenn said. "I guess Brad and I aren't tuned in enough to the vibrations around here."

"Well, there are plenty of vibrations around here to tune in to," Irene remarked. "Wow! This place is just drenched with psychic vibrations."

We were unable to chase down any of the clumps of glowing mist and observe any of them transform themselves into clear images of men and women. It may have been that, had our extrasensory receptors been tuned as finely as Irene's, we might have been able to see the psychic pictures much more clearly.

It appeared as though the sound portion of the ethereal broadcast had been received well enough, as several members of our midnight expedition insisted that they had heard the sounds of footsteps and brush being parted. But other than on Irene's super-set, the video portion of the program had been very blurred. All of us had seen the glowing, mist-like clumps, but none of us, other than the sensitive Mrs. Hughes, had been able to adjust the fine tune within our psyches enough to enable us to pick up a clear picture of the images that had been preternaturally recorded on the grounds of the old estate.

Earlier that day, Irene had walked around the estate with Mr. Roberts, the caretaker, and she had offered her psychic impressions of the former inhabitants of the Sumter place. We were unable to enter the home, because of the condition of the floors after several groups of vandals had struck the house to strip it of its valuable antiques.

The Sumter sisters, as well as their parents, had been real packrats and had never thrown anything away. According to Glenn's policeman friend, who had inspected the empty home during an early report of a mysterious light moving through the house and had seen the place before the vandals had looted it, the Sumters had never even disposed of newspapers and magazines, and the floors were stacked with nearly a century's worth of periodicals.

Here is a slightly edited transcript of Irene's psychic impressions of the old Sumter house in Iowa City:

Irene: I feel that they lived more in the upper rooms than in the lower. Is that correct?

Roberts: Yes, that's true.

Irene: I see an old woman dying in the house.

Roberts: Yes, that's correct.

Irene: The father had a mustache, wavy hair, and was meticulous with his personal records.

Roberts: Yes, absolutely. That's him.

Irene: One of the daughters was named Elizabeth.

Roberts: Yes.

Irene: The two daughters were different in every way, complete opposites.

Roberts: That is very true.

Irene: One left while she was quite young and married a man in uniform.

Roberts: Correct.

Irene: I receive a psychic impression that there were two rows of trees that once lined the driveway.

Roberts: Yes, that is so.

Irene: I get the name Floyd.

Roberts: That means nothing to me in relation to the house.

Irene: I feel that a lawyer spent a good deal of time in this house.

Roberts: That may well be so.

Irene: He was a big, jovial man, who liked to play chess with the father.

Roberts: I can't say yes or no to that.

Irene: Did they have plans to enlarge the house that were never carried out?

Roberts: Yes, I believe that there was some talk several years ago.

Irene: They especially planned to enlarge the library.

Roberts: That's very possible.

Irene: I feel that there have been three brides in this house, although one only stayed for a little while.

Roberts: I...I think that would be true.

Irene: The father was very violent verbally.

Roberts: That would probably be a fair characterization.

Irene: He kept some speckled hunting dogs.

Roberts: They always had a good many hunting dogs.

Irene: They also had a parrot.

Roberts: I was reared next door, and I remember, or seem to remember, that they had some kind of unusual bird when I was a boy. It may have been a parrot.

Irene: One of the daughters enjoyed painting and sketching.

Roberts: That's very true.

Irene: In her later years, she had to spend a lot of time in a wheel-chair.

Roberts: True.

Irene: The father liked to make things in a blacksmith shop.

Roberts: Yes, he kept a small shop in that shed out in back.

Irene: Really? Well, we haven't been out back yet, so I didn't see that.

Roberts: You wouldn't be able to tell it was a black-smith shop, anyway. It just looks like a shed now.

Irene: They raised guinea hens, did they?

Roberts: Yes, yes, they did.

Irene: I get the names Bullard and Wilson.

Roberts: Those names don't mean anything special to me, but the Sumters were always entertaining and having big parties.

Irene: The family liked to sing.

Roberts: Oh, yes! When I was a boy, many was the evening that we could hear them gathered around the piano singing away for all they were worth.

Irene: One of the daughters became very child-like as she grew older.

Roberts: Yes, that is true.

Irene: Oh, and I see that one of their prized possessions was a cabinet with carved legs and glass doors.

Roberts: Yes, that is correct.

Irene: Did they keep a family cemetery on the grounds?

Roberts: Yes, they did. It was supposed to be moved away when this part of town was annexed to the city, but there were rumors that they hadn't really complied with this ordinance.

Irene: Did you go over some legal papers with one of the daughters just before her death?

Roberts: Yes, I did.

Irene: Was the name Claude important to this family.

Roberts: Yes, it certainly was.

At first Mr. Roberts had been very skeptical of the idea of a psychic tromping about the grounds of the Sumter estate, seeking to pick up impressions from the past inhabitants. He had been quite reluctant to take time for such obvious foolishness, and it had taken a good measure of Glenn McWane's persuasive abilities to convince the caretaker that he should bother with us at all.

It was most interesting to watch Mr. Robert's obvious change of attitude as his exchange with Irene Hughes brought him deeper and deeper into a mysterious territory whose boundaries he had never before dreamed of transgressing. He knew that there had been no way in which Mrs. Hughes could have gained any information about the house and its inhabitants.

All Glenn knew of the house was that some policemen had seen strange lights moving around inside. Neither Glenn nor myself had researched the Sumter house in any manner whatsoever and it is doubtful that even the most exhaustive search of public records would have turned up the personal minutiae that Irene Hughes had siphoned from the psychic atmosphere of the old house.

The caretaker was, in a word, impressed, and I asked him afterward how he would assess Irene Hughes' percentage of accuracy in her statements about the Sumter' house.

He grinned, and his answer came quickly and easily. "I'd have to give her a ninety percent," he admitted, "and it would probably be higher if there was some way to check out every name she gave. Really, just about everything she said fit in. I don't know how, but she really knows what it's all about!"

A most irritating and eerie postscript to this case occurred approximately one calendar year after our psychic safari to this home when Glenn McWane and I were conducting follow-up research on the sites that had been visited by the seeress.

We pulled into the lane about midnight in the company of a number of other men and women. We took careful notice of a wire stretched across the lane. Someone, undoubtedly the caretaker, had strung a number of white and red strips of cloth from the line. We switched out the headlamps prepared to await the "something" which had been sighted by Glenn and a university professor just a few nights before.

Although we did not see the thing crossing the lane in its traditional spot, a column of light about the size of a human being appeared off to the right of the automobile. When Glenn snapped the headlamps on, we were startled to see a *three-tine pitchfork* a few feet in front of the station wagon.

I must confess that my attention had been directed to a spot further down the lane from the moment that we turned into the drive; therefore I cannot swear that the pitchfork had *not* been there before the headlamps were extinguished. Glenn, whose powers of observation are extremely acute, insists that the pitchfork was not there before he switched the headlamps back on bright. He is supported in this allegation by nearly everyone else who was in the party that night. All of us had to admit that we had not seen the pitchfork before the headlamps were restored to power.

Glenn argues that since the pitchfork had been driven into the ground just in back of the white and red stripes of cloth—and since everyone had commented upon this colorful addition to the environment—we would certainly have noticed such an obtrusive element as a pitchfork directly behind them. If that shimmering column of light truly planted that pitchfork before us, then I must admit that I cannot imagine a "memory pattern" being quite so animated.

the terrible
flying jelly bags

report made by two young men is the strangest of all the cases in the archives of the Swedish Defense Staff. According to Hans Gustafsson and Stig Rydberg, nightmarish creatures from a flying saucer attacked them and tried to kidnap them on the morning of December 20, 1958.

Fantastic as the story sounds, two psychologists, who conducted extensive tests with the young men while they were under hypnosis, concluded that the two Swedes were telling what they considered to be the truth and that their story rested on an actual occurrence.

Detailed accounts of the alien attempt at kidnapping were carried in more than 70 European papers, including the *Svenska Dagbladet*, *Stockholf Tidnigen*, *Helsingborg Dagblad*, and the Swiss *Weltaumbote*.

A thick mist had slowed their speed to about 25 miles per hour that morning as they drove to Helsingborg from Hoganas. Just before 3:00 A.M., they had come to a clearing in the thick forest that lined both sides of the highway. It was there that they saw the mysterious light.

For all the ridicule and mental anguish to which they would later be subjected—not to mention a most horrifying experience—the two young Swedes have often wished that they had kept on driving.

But they did not. They felt compelled to investigate. They left their car and walked cautiously into the mist.

"We saw a strange disc," Hans Gustafsson told reporters and officials. "It was resting on legs about two feet long. It seemed to be made of a peculiar, shimmering light that changed color."

The men had had barely time to express their amazement when they were suddenly confronted by a number of "blobs." According to Hans and Stig, "they were like protozoa, just a bit darker than the mist, sort of a bluish color, hopping and jumping around the saucer like globs of animated jelly."

Before the Swedes had time to react to the creatures, the jelly bags were enveloping them and, with powerful suction-like force, were trying to pull them toward the saucer.

"The drag the things exerted was terrific," the men said later. "And they gave off such a terrible smell—like ether and burnt sausage."

Stig Rydberg told investigators that his right arm sank up to the elbow in one of the blobs. "It almost seemed as if the creatures could read my mind. They parried every move before I made it. Their strength was not so great as the technique with which they wielded it."

After several desperate moments of frantic struggle, Rydberg freed himself from the sucking jelly bags and ran for the car, with two of the pulsating globs in close pursuit. Flinging open the door, he slammed his arm against the car horn in the desperate hope that someone might hear the blare and come to their rescue.

The two young Swedes were saved by the horn.

The harsh blare that cut into the early morning mist seemed to have the effect of the sound of a rescuing cavalry's bugle on the quivering jelly-bags. Dropping Hans Gustafsson, whom they had stretched out horizontally as he clung tenaciously to a fence post, the protoplasmic creatures quickly retreated to the shimmering saucer and soared into the sky.

"As it shot upwards," the beleaguered companions noted, "it emitted a brilliant light and a piercing, high-pitched whistle."

Nearly exhausted with the incredible donnybrook in which they had just engaged, the two Swedes continued on their journey, each agreeing that they should keep the story to themselves.

"We knew that people would only laugh at us if we were to tell them this fantastic story," the men said later. "And the authorities would probably have us committed to an asylum. Besides, such publicity wouldn't do either of us any good."

But that terrible stench seemed to stay with Hans and Stig. It seemed to have scarred their nostrils with its terrible odor. And their insides felt as though they had been turned upside down.

"We endured it for three days," Hans told newsmen, "then we decided that we should see a physician. We were afraid that those monsters might have permanently damaged us in some way, perhaps internally."

The doctor, after a careful and puzzled examination of the two men, told them that he could find nothing wrong with either of them. But the horrid, piping whistle still vibrated in their ears, and they still seemed fouled by the vile scent that had been exuded by the grasping blobs. At last they decided to make a public statement of their experience and face up to the mockery and undesirable publicity which they knew was certain to follow such a declaration.

For twelve hours, Stig and Hans were questioned and examined by officials from the Swedish Defense Staff, psychologists, doctors, and police. The multiple barrage of questions was unable to find the young men in a single contradiction or inconsistency. They made an offer—which was quickly accepted—to take the experts and the press to the spot where they had seen the saucer and its nightmarish crew. There, still visible, were the indentations which the space vehicle's landing tripod had made in the soft soil of the clearing. The psychologists concluded that their examination, conducted under deep hypnosis, had indicated that the two companions had definitely been caught in some mysterious magnetic field.

Danish officials were allowed to participate in the interrogation of Hans and Stig when they declared that Denmark's files contained a similar harrowing experience that had been endured by a Danish lady.

Neither young man had believed in "wild stories about flying saucers" before they stopped to investigate that mysterious light in the clearing. Neither of them will ever doubt such tales again.

the strange disappearance
of thomas meehan

he strange disappearance of Thomas P. Meehan, a thirty-eight-
year-old Concord, California, attorney and a referee for the State
Department of Employment Appeals bureau, on February 1,
1963, would seem to suggest that a bizarre kind of distortion of Time
occurred in some mysterious manner.

Meehan left Eureka for Concord at about 2:00 P.M. He drove as
far as Myers Flat before he stopped to telephone his wife and complain that he felt ill. She told him to spend the night at a motel and
not try to drive through.

It is from this point on that the time sequence becomes most con-
fusing—all the more so when the startling climax of the day's events
is realized.

Approximately 5:00 P.M.—Meehan checked into the Forty Winks
Motel at Redway.

Approximately 6:00 P.M.—The attorney drove to the Southern
Humboldt Community Hospital at Garberville to see a doctor.

At 6:45 P.M.—Meehan told the nurse that he felt as if he were dead. While she was checking him in and before he had seen a doctor, Meehan disappeared.

At 7:00 P.M.—A Myers Flat couple told the highway patrol that they had seen the tail lights of a car on Highway 101 drive into the Eel River.

At 8:00 P.M.—Attorney Meehan was talking with Chip Nunnemaker, the owner of the Forty Winks, at the motel. Meehan asked the innkeeper: "Do I look like I'm dead? I feel like I've died and the whole world died with me." Nunnemaker noticed that Meehan's shoes and trouser cuffs appeared wet and muddy.

9:00 P.M.—Meehan went to his room.

9:30 P.M.—Motel employee Harry Young went to Meehan's room to tell him that the call he had put through to Mrs. Meehan could not be completed because a storm had disrupted telephone service. Young saw that Meehan had changed into a black suit and a white shirt.

10:45 P.M.—The highway patrol found Meehan's car submerged in the Eel River, its tail lamps still shining like beacon lights for the searchers. Skid marks indicated that the vehicle had gone off the highway at high speed. Officers found blood on top of the car. The right front window of the car was open. Meehan was nowhere in sight, but droplets of blood and muddy footprints led up the bank for thirty feet—then vanished.

No trace of Thomas Meehan was found. Then, nineteen days later, his body was discovered in the Eel River near Myers Flat, sixteen miles downstream from where Meehan's car had veered into the river. The evidence of the autopsy suggested that the attorney had survived the crash with a superficial head wound, then, later had died of drowning.

Did Thomas P. Meehan's illness and confused state of mind lead him to weave in and out of hospitals and motel rooms and into a cold and swirling river? Or did that same confused but powerful mind exert an influence upon Time and Space?

If Meehan's automobile went into the river at 7:00 P.M. (and it must have, since no other automobiles were reported missing or were ever found in the river on that date), then how did he appear back at the motel to chat for an hour (8:00–9:00 P.M.) with the owner? Chip Nunnemaker did take note of Meehan's muddy shoes and trouser cuffs and the attorney's repeated complaint that he felt as if he were dead. Employee Harry Young saw Meehan at 9:30 P.M. and observed that Meehan had changed out of his wet clothing. Had Nunnemaker and Young actually talked with a dead man?

Although Meehan did not disappear without a trace forever, he certainly did disappear and reappear all during the evening of February 1st; and after he was last seen by Harry Young in his motel room, Meehan's body was not found until February 20.

Meehan's car was seen to plunge into the Eel River at about the same time he was sitting in the hospital in Garberville waiting to see a doctor. The police found drops of blood and muddy footprints that led up the bank for thirty feet before they simply vanished. Could Meehan have made his way back to the Forty Winks Motel?

Or did Thomas Meehan actually die by drowning when his automobile went into the river at about 7:00 P.M? Could his ill and confused mind and the will to live have projected an image of himself to the nurse, to Nunnemaker, to Young while his actual physical shell floated lifeless in the Eel River?

The author Ambrose Bierce wrote a remarkable short story entitled "An Occurrence at Owl Creek Bridge." In this tale, a man sentenced to a war-time death by hanging from the girders of a bridge is able to visualize the rope breaking and an escape from his captors all in the split second of reality before the taut rope snaps his neck and snuffs out his life-spark. Could the dying Thomas Meehan have discovered the same relativity of Time and could his mind in an altered state of consciousness have manipulated manmade time in a manner that would confuse all those who insist on measuring the passage of moments by the movement of a clock hand? Could the dying Thomas Meehan have wavered between dimensions of Time, dimensions of being, and utilized the unfathomable power of mind to influence matter?

our own haunted farmhouse in iowa

As some of my readers may know, I grew up in a home in which we had continual paranormal manifestations, ranging from knockings, rappings, the sound of measured footsteps, and occasional materializations.

Among my earliest childhood memories are the man and the woman who would walk into my bedroom at night and stand at my bedside, looking down at me. The man wore a black suit and seemed of rather stern demeanor. The woman wore an old-fashioned dress with a lace collar. Assessing their appearance from photographs I saw much later in an old family album, I have decided that the couple was most likely my great-grandparents, who had lived in the farmhouse long before my birth.

Dimension of spirit had always been very much a part of my mother's life, and she permitted my sister and me to perceive the eerie manifestations as evidence that from time to time a greater reality can impinge upon our more limited physical reality.

These comments are intended to assure you that moving into a house with an unseen resident held no particular terror for me personally; yet, when I moved into a haunted farmhouse with my family, the subsequent occurrence did prove to be quite unsettling.

On the outside, the farmhouse was magnificent. It was a solid two-story dwelling with an inviting front porch and sat atop a grassy hill. It was flanked by majestic pines and backed by a dwindling number of oak and walnut trees, which soon surrendered to a cornfield. At the foot of the hill was a picturesque creek with a small but sturdy bridge. Across the lane from the barn was a cabin said to be one of the very oldest pioneer homes in the county. The sturdy Iowa farmhouse seemed an ideal home in which our family might attempt an experiment in country living.

Inside, however, it seemed another matter entirely. I first entered the home with my friend Komar, who is very psychically sensitive. "Someone died here," he stated bluntly as soon as we crossed the threshold into the dining room.

The woman whose home we in the process of purchasing appeared startled by my friend's immediate announcement. When Komar quickly added, "A man died in the room across from the kitchen," she became visibly upset.

Within a few days we had the whole story. Her father, who she called Papa, had in his day been a well-respected church and community leader. His "day" had been in the 1920s and 1930s, and he had steadily grown more reclusive and more strongly opposed to modern technology. Papa's distrust of modern times extended to storm windows, electric lights, and running water. Life with Papa had been a rugged existence.

He had yielded to electric lights sometime in the 1940s, and he loved to sit in his room and listen to the radio—one of his few concessions to the contemporary world around him. He had not permitted running water in his house during his lifetime, and the plumbing we now saw had been only recently installed. There still was no drinking water in the home, however, and if we did not wish to carry buckets from the spring near the barn, we would have to dig a well.

My objections to the farmhouse were out voted, and we were soon moving to the country to inhabit Papa's monument to the "good old days." I strongly felt a presence in the house, and I was concerned about the children, since the presence I detected did not seem to be a hospitable one.

Shortly before we were to move in, a cousin of the vacating family approached me with an amused smile. "Well, Brad, you should really be happy now. What more could a writer of all those spooky books want than a haunted house of his own?"

When I pressed him for details, he only shrugged. "The old man was a stubborn Norwegian when he was alive, and I guess he's just as stubborn now that he's passed on. You should have some interesting evenings ahead of you."

I evaluated the situation, and we had a problem. If we truly were dealing with the earthbound spirit essence of a man who had been a pious church leader and a fervent opponent of progress, just how would he take to a family moving into his home that was headed by a psychical investigator with four lively kids who would immediately begin playing stereos and television sets? And how would the impressionable psyches of the kids, aged eight to sixteen, respond if the spirit became antagonized?

I was the first to undergo an initiation at the hands of an invisible welcoming committee.

I was alone in the house on a Sunday morning having some tea and toast while I read the newspaper. My wife, Marilyn (who later died in 1982), had gone to the village to open the small retail store she managed. One moment things were as idyllic as they could be; the next, my tranquility was shattered by a violent explosion that seemed to come from the basement.

Fearing that the oil-burning furnace had somehow exploded, I opened the basement door, expecting the worst. I could hear what seemed to be the walls of stone and brick caving in on the washer, the dryer, and the other appliances. I expected to be met by billowing clouds of thick black smoke.

But the instant I stepped onto the basement landing all sounds of disturbance ceased. The furnace was undamaged. The walls stood firm and solid. There was no smoke or fire.

Before I could puzzle the enigma through, I was startled by the sound of yet another explosion coming from somewhere upstairs.

I had a terrible image of the old brick chimney collapsing, and then I was pounding my way up the stairs.

The attic was as serene as the basement had been. I shook my head in confusion as I studied the sturdy beams and the excellent workmanship that held the roof and the brick chimney firmly erect and braced. The house had been built by master carpenters and brick-layers. It could probably withstand a tornado, I thought to myself as I attempted to understand what was happening around me.

A massive eruption sounded from the basement again, creating the visual image of several hand grenades being triggered in rapid succession. I slammed the attic door behind me, fearing the awesome damage that surely must have occurred.

But before I could run back down the stairs to inspect the extent of the destruction, I heard what sounded like someone tap-dancing behind the door to my son Steven's room. I knew that Steven did not tap-dance and that I was home alone.

Then I thought of Reb, our beagle. I laughed out loud in relief. The sound of "tap dancing" had to be the clicking of the dog's paws on the wooden floor. Buy why wasn't Reb barking to be released? He was never shy about expressing his wishes, frustration, or irritation.

I hesitated with my hand on the doorknob. I felt an even greater hesitation when I heard Reb barking outside. The dog was out back, by the kitchen door. I was so engrossed in the mystery of the strange disturbances that I had forgotten I had let him out. It was cold out that morning, and Reb was barking to come into the warm house.

Who—what—was still merrily dancing behind the door to Steven's room?

I shamed myself for permitting fear to make me lose control of my hand. I twisted the knob and pushed open the door.

The room was empty. And the dancing stopped as suddenly as the explosions had when I had swung wide the basement and attic doors.

I suddenly felt as though I were being scrutinized by a dozen or more pairs of eyes.

Another detonation roared up at me from beyond the basement.

I sensed a game plan behind all of this. I was now supposed to dash down the stairs in puzzled panic, desperately seeking the cause the violent "explosions." I could almost hear the giggles of unseen pranksters.

I resolved not to play the silly game any more. I walked purposefully back to the kitchen table, where I had left my tea, toast, and Sunday newspaper.

Then it sounded as if the attic roof were being torn from its anchoring beams. The basement walls shuddered and collapsed in what seemed to be another explosion.

During my career as a psychical researcher I had become well versed in the games that certain entities like to play with people. I decided to do my best to ignore the phenomena.

The tap dancing was nearer now. It was coming from the music room, the room that the previous owners had kept locked and unused—Papa's room. I had place the piano, television and stereo in the room and had repainted the walls and ceiling. I had blessed the room and announced that it would henceforth be a place of love and laughter.

I was determined not to glance up from my newspaper, even if Papa, a headless horseman, or a snarling troll came walking out of the music room. I was not going to play the game.

Within about twenty minutes the disturbances had stopped. I was relieved that I had guessed the secret. It appeared that the invisible pranksters did not enjoy playing tricks on someone who remained indifferent to such a grand repertoire of mischief.

Since I did not wish to alarm the rest of the family and was totally immersed in working on a new book at my office in the village, I did not mention the incident to anyone.

About three nights later, when I was working late at my office, I receive an urgent telephone call from my older son, Bryan. The panic in the sixteen-year-old's voice told me that I must drive out to the farmhouse at once.

When I arrived, I found Bryan barricaded in his room, together with Reb and a .12-gauge shotgun. After I had calmed the boy I learned that Bryan too had fallen victim to the tricksters.

Bryan had been alone at home watching television in the music room. He heard what he assumed was the sound of other family members returning home. He listened to the familiar noises of an automobile approaching, car doors slamming, voices and laughter, and the stomping of feet on the front porch.

Then he was surprised to hear loud knocking at the front door. Everyone in the family had their own keys, so why would anyone knock? And why would they be pounding at the front door when they usually entered through the back door, in the kitchen?

Bryan begrudgingly stirred himself from his television program and went to admit whoever it was on the front porch. He was astonished to find it empty.

Just as he was about to step outside in an attempt to solve the mystery, he heard knocking at the back door. Uttering a sigh of frustration, Bryan slammed the front door and began to head for the kitchen. He had taken no more than a few steps when the knocks were once again at the front door.

By now Bryan knew that someone was playing a joke on him. He turned on the yard light so that he could identify the jokesters' automobile. He gasped when he saw that his car was the only one there.

Fists were now thudding on both doors, and Reb was going crazy, growling and baring his teeth.

Bryan next became aware of an eerie babble of voices and short bursts of laughter. Someone very large was definitely leaning against the kitchen door, attempting to force it open.

That was when he called me. A few seconds of hearing my son's strained, frightened voice and the angry snarls of the dog in the background convinced me that something was very wrong.

"Dad," Bryan told me, "Reb and I are in my room. Someone is coming up the stairs. I can hear him move up one step at a time!"

An intuitive flash informed me what was occurring. The invisible pranksters were playing games again.

"Bry, your fear is feeding it," I advised my son. "It has already tried the game with me. Try to stay calm. Put on some music. Distract your mind. I'm on my way home right now!"

It had snowed earlier that day, and I prayed for no ice and no highway patrolman. I was fortunate in both respects and managed to shave four minutes from the normal twelve-minute drive to the farmhouse.

The doors were locked from the inside, and Bryan was still barricaded in his room with Reb. I offered silent thanks that the boy hadn't blown any holes in himself or the walls with the shotgun.

I showed Bryan that there were no footprints in the freshly fallen snow. There was no evidence of tire tracks in the lane. No human had visited him, I explained, but rather some nonphysical intelligences that would initiate a spooky game with anyone who would play along with them.

Early the next evening I gave my children instructions on how best to deal with any ghostly mechanisms of sound or sight that might frighten them.

Basically the strategy was to remain as indifferent and as aloof to the disturbances as possible. In a good-natured way one should indicate that he or she simply does not wish to play such silly games.

Under no circumstances should one become defiant or angry or threatening. The laws of polarity would only force the tricksters into coming back with bigger and spookier tricks in response to the negative energy that had been directed toward them.

Whether we were dealing with poltergeists, restless spirits in limbo, or a repository of unknown energy that somehow mimicked human intelligence, I felt that I had given the kids some advice that was sound.

Bryan had experienced the phenomenon firsthand, so he was now better prepared to confront it should the situation arise. Steven had already intellectualized the occurrences and found them fascinating. My daughter, Kari, who had strong mediumistic abilities, seemed aware of the disturbances but remained strangely aloof from them.

It was all a little too awesome for eight-year-old Julie to understand, however. Whenever she was left alone in the farmhouse, the entities would gang up on her, and I would return to find her standing at the end of the lane or seeking refuge in a neighbor's home. In each instance she complained of having heard strange voices, laughter, and weird music.

One night just as I entered my office, I heard the telephone ringing. It was Julie. She had been calling the office ever since I had left home and was in tears. A dramatic manifestation had begun within minutes after I had left her at the kitchen table, eating cookies and drinking milk.

This time it had begun with laughter from the music room. There was a noisy blur of voices, as if several people were trying to speak at once. Then came some "funny piano music" and the sound of a drum.

Valiantly Julie had tried to practice what I had told her do: to remain calm, act aloof, and not to play the game with whatever it is that likes to play such spooky tricks on people.

When the rhythmic tapping of the drum suddenly gave way to blaring horns and trumpets, Julie's indifference melted.

I had not been gone for more than two or three minutes, but Julie knew that I was headed for the office. She just let the telephone ring until I answered it.

Not long ago Julie, now thirty, and I recalled the incidents that she had experienced in the eerie old farmhouse. Interestingly enough, Julie finally had identified the music she had heard coming from the music room on the several occasions she had been left alone.

"When I was a senior in high school," she said, "some girlfriends and I were just driving around one night, and we had on one of those radio stations that play nostalgic music from the 'good old days.' We were talking about how different some of the music used to be, when suddenly I just about freaked out. It was a good thing that I wasn't driving! It was the same music that I had heard coming from that spooky room, and all those terrible memories came back to me."

Julie had heard Glenn Miller's "In the Mood."

Incredibly it had been music from the 1940s that had so frightened Julie. To this day, whenever she hears Benny Goodman, Duke Ellington, or Glenn Miller, she gets a cold shiver, for it was their old records that she had heard playing from the darkened recesses of the music room.

Although she grew up in a home where we enjoyed eclectic musical taste, I must confirm that the tunes of the 1940s would have been foreign to Julie at that time of her life. The family had classical, folk, motion-picture themes, rock, pop, and Broadway show tunes, but we had no big-band records from the 1940s in our collection.

Now that she was older, I shared with Julie what I knew about the music room. Papa had been a strong-willed man who didn't care much for progress—not even running water in the house. And he never would have approved of his daughter and her husband selling the place. He had died in that room, and they had kept it locked and had never used it again while they lived there, since things just hadn't felt right in there.

Papa might not have cared much for most of the instruments of progress, but he must have accepted radio. And he probably tolerated the music of the 1940s, the years when he would have been having some of the most meaningful experiences of his life.

Or maybe the invisible tricksters just loved to jitterbug.

meŋ aŋd womeŋ wĥo walk tĥrougĥ doorwaўs to otĥer dimeŋsioŋs

n February of 1971, shortly after an article of mine on time travel had appeared in *Saga* magazine, I received a letter from an unusually talented gentleman named Al Kiessig, who claimed the ability to walk through "doorways" between dimensions. In subsequent correspondence, Kiessig shared numerous experiences with me. I found my correspondent to be an open-minded, sincere man. The reader, of course, will have to judge for himself as to the validity of the following experiences.

In Kiessig's terminology, it was in Missouri that he found the "West Door," the door of evil, and the "East Door," the entrance into the Spirit World. According to Al Kiessig: "At the West Door, the wanderers of the spirit world can leave and enter our world clothed so as to be seen as one of us—and no human eye can detect the difference.

"There are two places, one in Missouri and one in Arkansas, where I walked into this next door neighbor of ours. It is very silent. It looks like our world, but there is no sound, no wind, no sun, even though it looks like the sun is shining.

"In the state of Missouri I found two fields that had doors, or what I call 'vortexes.' No matter where you walked you would come back to your starting place, and if you hit the center of the vortex, then you would come out from a mile to two miles beyond the place you entered in a section that would be unrecognizable to you until you stopped and regained your inner balance. Then the surroundings would gradually become familiar.

"Each door is different, but it is my belief that if one could recognize these door openings, one could pick the door in Arkansas that would permit me to step into your front yard in Iowa.

"In December of 1965, my wife and I moved back to Arkansas. Shortly thereafter, I left the house about 9:30 A.M. one morning to walk with my dog along two sides of a 40-acre field. I walked to the corner directly opposite the house up on the side of a steep hill. From that corner to the road was three quarters of one side of the 40-acre square, and as it took me about 45 minutes to get to that corner, there was no reason why I should not have been back to the house before noon.

"So I started walking along the fence. I walked up one hill and down another, paying no attention to anything but the fence. Then I stopped to rest and my dog came to me. From then on, he stayed close to my side, which was odd for him. I was walking slowly, since I have emphysema and I have no wind to speak of.

"Then I noticed the quiet. No shadows. No wind. I said to myself that I would walk to the top of the hill so that I could see just where I was.

"When I finally reached the top, I saw a fenced-in hayfield. Less than three quarters of a mile away there were two wooden frame, two-story houses. Each house had the usual accumulation of stuff in the yards, but there were no cars or garages. There was a mud or gravel road in front of each house. One house appeared to me to be facing south with a road running east and west. The other house was facing me with a road running north and south. These roads did not connect.

"There was no sign of life. There was no smoke from the chimneys. All this time Joe, my dog, stood there looking at me. So when I said, 'Let's go back the way we came,' he was one happy dog.

"It wasn't until we got to that strange corner that we felt the breeze and heard the crows and other birds. We were glad to be back. I walked to the house the short way, because I knew it would be about 12:30 P.M., and I would be a half-hour late.

"When I was nearly to the house, I noticed that the winter sun was only about two hours from setting. I was amazed to see that the clock in the house said 3:30 P.M.!

"In Missouri I found a number of places where one could stop his car while driving and have his body pains chased away.

"There was a place on the acreage that we were renting that healed the painful areas of your body just according to how you lay down and in what position you were in.

"In the region of the Ozarks, it was nothing for me to see into this other dimension. I could not enter, but I could see into it, as if through a large window. And I could see the people, *live* people, who entered our world or dimension, using the same mode of transportation so as not to give themselves away as aliens.

"Who are *they*? As much as I have probed into this, the only thought that comes to me more often than other theories, is that this other dimension is the 'Hell on Earth' where Jesus went to preach for the three days before he ascended into Heaven.

"I have entered these 'doorways' while driving and saved myself hundreds of miles of driving. Unfortunately, the reverse has also happened to me.

"Some of these doors to other dimensions open like an elevator door with no elevator there to step into. Others open into a land of no life. Some take you back into the past, and some take you into the future on this world. Then there are doors that open into chambers that send the body to a distant star.

"This world we know as Earth is not the only world inhabited by people like us. We must keep our minds open wide.

"There is no way that I can prove any of the events stated in this letter," Kiessig closed in one of his long letters to me. "My word, which is well known hereabouts to be good as gold, must do."

Is it possible that some men and women may have a peculiar psychic make-up which permits them to transgress the boundaries between this plane of reality and other dimensions?

Can these men and women be possessed of abilities which enable them to travel to realms of being normally unobtainable to those in the physical body?

Or are these only personal hallucinations created out of some psychic need within certain personality types?

As Al Kiessig admitted, he had only his word to substantiate his claims, and even though his friends and neighbors in Arkansas might swear by his promises and his oaths, such testimonials do not stand up well under the critical scrutiny of the scientific testing laboratory.

In several cases of "interdimensional intervisitation," however, there exist enough witnesses to take the experience out of the subjective and place it into the evidential.

In 1953, a schoolboy in the Philippines was seen by many to disappear from closed rooms, then, incredibly, to reappear in another section of his city of Manila. In 1965, *United Press International* correspondent Vicente Maliwang interviewed Cornelio Closa, the famous "Invisible boy," who was then a twenty-five-year-old married man, the father of two children, in order to record his impressions of the astounding events which had taken place in his life thirteen years before.

Journalist Maliwang and his photographer Eduardo Martinez managed to speak with Cornelio in the presence of his father, a twenty-three-year-old sister, and an eighteen-year-old brother. Cornelio admitted that he was hesitant about repeating his story, especially in the company of strangers.

"If you told me the same story," he smiled, "I wouldn't believe you, either. I would laugh in your face!"

Before he fully relaxed for the interview, Cornelio asked that his wife remove their children from the home. "My wife knows the story," he said, "but the children wouldn't understand. Besides, I would be just as happy if I could forget that it ever happened. It seems like a frightful dream, a nightmare. But I know it happened and nothing can ever change that fact."

The strange, frightful dream began for Cornelio in September of 1951 when he was a sixth-grader at the Zamora elementary school. One day he met a beautiful girl dressed in white with long blonde hair reaching down to her waist. She was barefoot, about Cornelio's age, but the boy noticed she floated, rather than walked, when she moved beside him.

Although the girl did not open her smiling lips, Cornelio was able to "hear and understand" what she said. When she touched his hand, he felt different, very light. He became unaware of his surroundings.

"I don't remember anymore what else happened during that first meeting," he said, "but I went home later and did not tell anybody of my experience."

The beautiful blonde girl came often. Cornelio remembered that the things around him looked real and natural, but somehow he had the feeling that *he* was no longer real.

"There were many times when the girl and I would float around and go to many places in the city," Cornelio told the reporter. "We went many times to movie houses and visited the International Fair that was being held in the city. When I was with her, I didn't feel exhausted or hungry."

The strangest thing, Cornelio recalled, was that nobody seemed to notice them.

Soon, Cornelio's schoolteacher complained to his parents that he had been skipping school. Father Closa put the law down to his son, but even an enforced march to school would not prevent the ethereal girl from snatching the boy away from his classroom.

The girl would appear before him in school. She would hold out her hand. Cornelio would feel some "sensation," then there would be no other thought in his mind but to go with her.

"Even with the door closed," Cornelio remembered, "I was able to go through it, just be walking through it as if it were open. Then I would hear my classmates shouting, 'Cornelio is gone!'"

At home, the Closa family would lock all the doors and windows, but to absolutely no avail.

"I kept on seeing the girl and I was able to go out with her despite the closed doors," Cornelio said. 'Sometimes I would be gone as long as three days, although I had no knowledge of my own how long I had been away."

Finally his despairing parents sent Cornelio to a mental institution, then to a welfare institution. Authorities said that he was a nor-

mal boy who would be better off living with his parents, so Cornelio was sent home. The drastic measure had accomplished the cessation of the strange girl's visitations to the young boy, however.
Two pastors added to the separation by intense prayers, and Cornelio's nightmare was at an end.

Although we are pleased to learn that Cornelio Closa is now able
to lead a normal life, we are still left with the great mystery—where
had he been? Was the beautiful blonde girl, who communicated with
him through telepathy and who floated with him invisibly through
the air, an actual citizen of some other dimension, or was she but a
projection of his own psyche, an externalization projected to help
him deal with his amazing talent of dematerializing his body?

One would write the schoolboy's experiences off to an energetic
imagination and a passion for mischief—or at best to a series of out-
of-body experiences—if it were not for the fact that he did disappear
from closed classrooms, surrounded by classmates and teacher, and
locked doors and windows, ringed in by members of his family.

Michael Helferty of Picton, Ontario, Canada, saw no lovely
blonde girl beckoning with outstretched hand, but neither can he
nor anyone else explain *where* he went for five days.

The thirteen-year-old Helferty was last seen walking along Lake
Street toward Outlet Beach to go swimming on July 30, 1960. Then
he disappeared.

By the time he was found sleeping in a nest of grass alongside
the Canadian National Railway tracks west of Picton five days later,
his frantic parents had posted a five-hundred-dollar reward for information on his whereabouts and police, friends, and volunteer
searchers had painstakingly combed the area.

Michael was unaware that any more than a few hours had passed
since he set out to go swimming, and he had no memory of where
he had been. He showed no signs of exposure, sunburn, hunger,
or thirst. He was fresh and alert and not the least bit tired. The
Helferty family physician declared him well-nourished, well-cared
for, and clean. Strangely enough, his clothes were perfectly dry, even
though there had been a heavy dew during the night.

The only thing at all unusual was that Michael was wearing his
swim trunks, rather than his underwear, under his trousers. Since

he had set out to go swimming with his trunks in his hand, it appears that he at least may have entered the water.

Michael himself found it difficult to believe that he had "lost" five days, and he insisted that he had no knowledge or memory of where he had been.

His father could only shake his head and utter: "It's a mystery, but somebody's taken care of him, that's for sure."

Michael Helferty swore that he had no conscious memory of where he had spent his strange five-day vacation. Little Kathy Cramer may have remembered where she disappeared to, but she was not telling anyone.

The six-year-old girl disappeared from her home on Park Street in Wood's Hole, Massachusetts, about 7:00 P.M. on August 15, 1960. Local police officers, state police, firemen, a crew of volunteers, and two police bloodhounds meticulously scoured a two-mile area, while a Coast Guard vessel patrolled the adjacent water front. At 9:00 P.M. two hundred airmen from nearby Otis Air Force Base initiated a search-march for the missing Kathy Cramer.

It goes without saying that the Cramer household was carefully searched before the original alarm concerning Kathy's absence had been issued. In addition, Falmouth Deputy Police Chief Antone Morgardo and Rev. Wilkin J. Kingwell, rector of St. John's Church in Newtonville, testified that they had carefully explored the house three times. Yet, incredible as it may seem, the six-year-old object of the massive search was found at 3:00 A.M., peacefully sleeping on her bed.

When gratefully weeping yet stunned and incredulous parents asked Kathy where she had been, the six-year-old stubbornly announced that she was not telling.

Stern police officers, solicitous neighbors, coaxing relatives all got the same answer: "I'm not telling!"

Had some kidnapper decided better of his dangerous gambit and returned the child, desperately making a game of it all with her, making her promise not to tell where they had been?

Or had some cosmic, interdimensional being removed the child for a time for some purpose of his own, then brought her back to our plane of reality with a promise not to betray the "Good Fairy's" secret?

There may be a number of other possible explanations, but one that we should consider is that the child herself may have discovered the marvelous, albeit awesome, secret of psychically "crawling" through the cracks and crevices between spheres of existence.

In the June, 1959, issue of *Fate* magazine, writer Keith Ayling recounted one of the Paris *Surete's* (France's counterpart of the FBI) most mystifying unsolved cases. The puzzling crime involved the apparent ability of a man to make mock of Time and Space.

The incident concerned the disappearance of a valuable painting from the home of M. Pierre Dubois in April, 1929. Police could find no fingerprints, no signs of a forced entry, no clues to the method used to spirit away a $50,000 painting from under the very noses of the Dubois family and their five servants.

Two days after the painting had been stolen, M. Dubois received a telegram from his son, Captain Marcel Dubois, the well-known French toxicologist, who was working for the army in Algiers. Captain Dubois wished to know if his favorite painting still hung in the dining room.

M. Dubois was irritated that word of the picture's theft had leaked out, although he was puzzled by what means his son in Algiers might know of their loss when they had so carefully managed to keep word of the painting's disappearance out of the Paris newspapers. Resigned to his son's recriminations, M. Dubois tele- grammed:

"Picture has been stolen. Police working on case. Surete expects to recover same. Papa."

When Captain Dubois received the return message, be was not angry with his father for being careless with the precious painting. He knew that his own yearning to once more physically possess his work of art was responsible for that painting to have materialized on the pink stucco wall of his apartment in Algiers. He also knew that he was not mad, because he had had the district commissioner, the local postmaster, and fellow doctor verify the painting's presence.

According to Captain Dubois, it had been Abdul Oab, the head of the Arab village where he had been giving inoculations, who had convinced him of the power of the mind.

For purposes of demonstration, the Arab had asked Dubois to think of something in Paris that he would very much like to have with him in Algiers. Dubois thought of the picture in his father's dining room, because it was the thing he had most admired in his youth.

At Abdul Oab's bidding, Captain Dubois turned around to behold the same painting on the stucco wall behind him.

The Arab told the Frenchman that there were conditions. Captain Dubois might possess the painting for only forty-eight hours. Then the painting had to return to Paris where it belonged.

In the presence of Captain Dubois' three friends, Abdul asked the young doctor if he believed that the picture could be sent back. Dubois nodded his affirmation. The Arab raised his hand and the wall was instantly blank.

According to Ayling: "The next morning, Dubois received another telegram from his father. The picture had been restored to its place on the wall of the Dubois dining room. The police had been informed."

Parisian newspapers suggested numerous theories to explain the enigma, ranging from poltergeists and practical jokers to an elaborately staged hoax to boost the value of the painting.

Dr. Alexander Canon, M.D., a noted author and authority on psychic phenomena, accredited the incident to a demonstration of the yogi power of *maya* which, according to Dr. Canon, "works on the mind in such a way that people are able to manifest what they visualize."

"One thing is certain," Ayling assures us, "this strange thing happened, and the Paris police, the French newspapers, and the *London Times* reported it."

Mrs. Frank L. Nickerson of Seattle, Washington, told of her meeting with a young man who seemed to possess the ability to control his environment in yet another way (December 1953, *Fate* magazine). According to Mrs. Nickerson, in March of 1949, her husband had a job crewing ships. He came to know one young man quite well, a slender, slight blond named Donald.

One night as the three of them were visiting, Mrs. Nickerson offered to take Donald's picture. The young man laughed and told her that no one could take a picture of him. Mrs. Nickerson prided herself on her ability as a photographer, and she became impatient, thinking that Donald meant that he had never seen anyone take a good picture of himself.

"But I mean it," Donald warned her as she carefully checked the light and her camera. "No one can take my picture. There will be nothing on the film."

Mrs. Nickerson snapped two pictures of their friend. Later, when she picked up the prints, she found that the photographs of her husband, sitting in the same chair with the same lighting, had turned out perfectly; but the two negatives of Donald had turned out completely blank.

In her conclusion, Mrs. Nickerson writes that Donald "seemed to avoid us after that." Did their young friend avoid them for fear that they might begin to realize a certain bizarre truth about him?

Who might these "angels" or "devils" be who walk about in our very midst, while we either entertain or reject them, totally unaware of their true nature or their true purpose?

Joseph Kerska of San Francisco told of the incident involving seventeen-year-old Carmen Chaney one hot summer day in Fresno, California, in 1936 (*Fate*, January, 1961). It would seem that the old woman observed by Miss Chaney and several others was not a confused and innocent space traveler, but a deliberate and aware dimension-hopper.

Carmen Chaney first noticed the strange old lady in black as she crossed Tyler Street at the intersection. The old woman moved slowly, with difficulty, as if her legs were not functioning properly. Assuming that the lady must be ill, Carmen and her aunt Frankie ran out into the street to help her.

When the old lady saw the two solicitous women approaching her, her reaction was far from that of relief at sighting succor on the way. In fact, she reacted with panic, as if she wanted no one to approach her.

Kerska writes: "Only 20 feet from her now, they were fascinated by her large, blazing eyes, set deep in a chalk-white face, the skin of which appeared to be stretched tightly over her skull. She was about four feet, 10 inches tall, thin and scrawny; snow white hair showed in wisps under her large black hat; she wore a high-necked, long-sleeved dress and high button shoes of a decade gone by. The black of her hair which was pulled down low over her face, as well as that of her dress, was old to the point of decay, as both had turned greenish. She carried no bag or purse. Altogether she was a pathetic figure."

By now several of the neighbors on the block were watching the strange old lady retreating from the two well-meaning young women. The old lady hobbled into an alley, then she looked around helplessly, as she realized that more than thirty people were intently observing her bizarre behavior.

"She stopped for a brief moment," Kerska said in *Fate*, "then she vanished! Disappeared in the blink of an eyelash!"

The many witnesses to the fantastic disappearance excitedly exchanged opinions and speculations. Police officers who were summoned to the scene chose to believe that the old woman had been ill and had simply stumbled out of sight of her observers. But an extensive search of the alley and the houses on either side "...revealed nothing, and the police, after a number of sarcastic comments, drove away."

It is easy to make sarcastic comments when one is dealing with such bizarre, inexplicable phenomena as the fate of disappearing people. Sarcasm comes readily to the tongue when such reports are related by even the sincere and the respectable members of our society. But demeaning the phenomenon contributes nothing toward explaining the phenomenon.

Whether there truly are "holes" and "doorways" between dimensions of reality, whether there may exist kidnappers from other planes of being, whether swirling vortexes and triangles of terror may snatch up ships and planes and their crews and send them spinning into another Space-Time continuum, and whether there may actually exist uniquely talented men and women who can "will" themselves in and out of dimensional "windows" must at this time be considered possible, but unproved.

This author only wonders how many people, ships, and planes must vanish under mysterious circumstances before the practitioners of orthodox science will weaken enough to permit themselves to become seriously interested in the elusive hows and whys of strange disappearances.

On August 6, 1970, the Caldwell, New Jersey, *Progress* carried a story about a mysterious "silver thread" that hung in the sky over the city. The *Progress* maintained that the thread was no illusion.

"Too many people, including policemen and reporters have caught sight of it to deny its existence," the newspaper stated. "To some it looks like strand from a giant cobweb stretching off into the clouds...

"It looks rigid, as if it were a wire, not a string. It appears silver when the sunlight strikes it. On Monday it hung about 150 feet above the houses on Forest Avenue and Hillside Avenue...

"The Caldwell police tried to trace it on Monday, found signs of it up Hillside and down toward West Caldwell, but lost it in the clouds before tracking down the origin...

"The mystery of the silver thread among the clouds has yet to be solved. It all looks perfectly innocent and harmless—but where does it come from, where does it go, and why?"

John A. Keel, noted ufologist and author of numerous provocative books (i.e. *Our Haunted Planet*), traveled to Caldwell to investigate the phenomenon, along with such investigators as Dr. Berthold Schwarz. They found that the "silver thread" had been visible periodically throughout the month of August. The line could not have been dangling from some out-of-sight kite or balloon, because it remained stationary.

Dr. Schwarz learned that on the afternoon of August 31, Mrs. A.P. Smith had heard a noise like a loud thunderclap, which she thought was a jet breaking the sound barrier. Later, she noticed that a section of the "silver thread" had fallen to the ground.

Honoring a promise to Keel, Mrs. Smith obtained a specimen for the investigator, then she called the police and delivered the rest of the thread into their hands.

Writing in Vol. II, No. 3, of the *INFO Journal*, Keel found that the substance appeared to be nylon fishline. However, when he visited a kite store in New York City to compare it with the strings being sold, he was unable to match it with any of the types available.

"It is quite stiff, more like a fiber from a plastic broom, and is translucent," Keel reported.

INFO's editorial comment was to quote Charles Fort's statement: "I think we're fished for."

But we still don't know who is dong the fishing and whether our people who disappear under strange circumstances are, in dreadful reality, being "landed" in the nets of some interdimensional fisherman.

Let he who would scoff at such fanciful, yet fearsome, theories step forward and jerk the silver line that dangles above New Jersey.

people, animals, and things that fall into other dimensions

On June 3, 1968, Dr. and Mrs. Gerardo Vidal attended a family reunion at the home of Señor Rapallini in Chascomus, a town situated near National Route 2 in Buenos Aires province, Argentina. The Vidals arrived in the late afternoon, partook of a lavish dinner, then began the drive back to their residence at Maipu. Another couple, who happened to be both near neighbors in Maipu and relatives attending the same celebration, decided to leave at the same time as the Vidals.

The two cars set out on Route 2 just a few minutes before midnight. The first couple arrived back in Maipu without incident, but they waited for the Vidals to show up before continuing on to their home. After they had waited for several minutes, they began to fear that the Vidals might have met with an accident.

They discussed the matter for but a few more moments, then they decided to get back into their automobile and retrace the route back to Chascomus in order to look for the Vidals. Although the hour was late, their concern for their relatives outweighed considerations

79

for their own comfort. But strangely enough, they traveled the entire eighty miles back to the Rapallinis without seeing a trace of the Vidals or their automobile.

Deciding against staying the night in Chascomus, they set out once again on Route 2 to Maipu. This time they strained their eyes at virtually every foot of the highway in an attempt to see down the steep banks. They returned to Maipu without having seen a trace of the Vidals. A telephone call to the Maipu hospital informed them that no accidents had been reported that night.

The Vidals had disappeared without a trace and without a clue.

Then, forty-eight hours later, Senor Rapallini received a long-distance telephone call from the Argentine consulate in Mexico City, Mexico. It was Dr. Vidal.

Incredulously, Rapallini listened to his friend asking him to remain calm and not to worry about them. He and his wife were both safe and unharmed. They would be flying back to Buenos Aires, and Dr. Vidal gave him the date and hour of their arrival so that they might be met at the airport.

Astonished friends and relatives gathered to meet the plane from Mexico City. Dr. Vidal emerged from the airplane wearing the same clothes that he had been wearing on the evening of their mysterious disappearance. Mrs. Vidal was taken directly from the airport to a private clinic, the victim of a "violent nervous crisis."

Dr. Vidal had been admonished by the consulate not to issue any public statements about their strange "teleportation" from the province of Buenos Aires to Mexico, but he did relate enough details of the bizarre journey for the newspaper *La Razon* to put together a story made up of comments from Dr. Vidal and interviews with the Vidals' friends and relatives.

A correspondent in Argentina sent this author copies of the various reports printed in *La Razon*, and the eerie account has been translated as follows:

Dr. Vidal and his wife left the city of Chascomus a few minutes before midnight and were traveling on Route 2. They were listening to the radio and driving at a speed which would permit them to keep the tail lights of their friends' automobile always in view.

They were just outside the suburbs of Chascomus when the Vidals' automobile became enveloped in a dense fog bank. He slowed down. The Vidals became aware only of blackness.

The next thing Dr. and Mrs. Vidal knew was that it was suddenly bright daylight and they were on an unfamiliar road. When Dr. Vidal stepped out of the car to investigate the situation, he was amazed to discover that every bit of paint had been scorched off the automobile's surface.

Dr. Vidal flagged down a passing motorist to ask directions. Completely nonplussed, he returned to his wife to tell her that the man had said that they were outside of Mexico City, another continent and several thousand miles away from their home. Later, in the Argentine consulate, they had to accept another startling fact: their blackout during the strange trip had lasted for forty-eight hours.

"In spite of the halo of fantasy that the story of the Vidals seems to wear," *La Razon* commented, "there are certain details which do not cease to preoccupy even the most unbelieving: The entrance of Vidal's wife into a Buenos Aires clinic; the proved arrival of the couple on an airplane that arrived nonstop from Mexico; the disappearance of the car; the intervention of the consulate; the serious attitude of the police in Maipu in regard to the event; and the telephone call from Mexico to the Rapallini—which was confirmed by *La Razon*—to make all of this acquire the status of a matter worthy of being considered in these times of space adventures and fantastic appearances of flying saucers."

In a follow-up to the strange account of the Vidals' experience, *La Razon* interviewed Professor Alejandro Eru, secretary of the Argentine College of Parapsychology, for his remarks on the peculiar case. Eru, professor of humanities at the University of La Plata, responded by providing the reporter with three similar cases of unexplainable transportations.

"A man who lived near Bahia Blanca suffered a dizziness when a strange aerial craft appeared before him," Professor Eru said. "Ten minutes later, he came to, but found himself in Salta, one of the northernmost provinces in Argentina. The authorities in both locales communicated with each other immediately, and the man's automobile was found in Bahia Blanca in exactly the spot where he claimed it would be."

The second case Professor Eru delineated for the journalist involved a professor of law on the faculty at Santos."This man claimed that a flying disc had sucked him aboard and had taken him on a fantastic aerial journey before it released him," Professor Eru said.

Communicating entities were involved in the third case history the professor presented to *La Razon*.

"This experience involves a most widely known and highly responsible painter, sculptor, and theatrical artist, whose initials are B.S.P.," Eru noted. "For many years, he was the director of the Art Salon of the Municipal Bank.

"B.S.P. testified that he had been contacted by a blond Nordic-appearing man who had eyes so clear that he appeared blind. The blond spoke in a guttural, unintelligible language, but his mannerisms were friendly. The artist got only a glimpse of the inside of the entity's craft before a wave of dizziness engulfed him.

"When he awakened," Professor Eru went on, "B.S.P. saw that he was flying along with three blond beings. One of them, very gentle, interrogated him in a language also unintelligible, but B.S.P. understood, or at least believed he perceived the man's thoughts by telepathic communication.

"B.S.P. was told not to be frightened; they would return him to Earth in precisely the same spot from which they had plucked him. B.S.P. said that all during the fight be was in a kind of swoon, but he believed that he saw beneath him the terrain of Japan, France, and, later, Chile. When he awakened from the peculiar trance state, he found himself to be standing in exactly the same spot at which he had first encountered the blond being."

In a summation for *La Razon*, Professor Eru said: "In none of these cases do the witnesses speak of hallucinations. Nor do they speak of having been intoxicated or doped. What caused these phenomena? Well, unfortunately, we cannot answer that conclusively. It may be that 'friends' from other worlds possess some type of electromagnetic wave with which they attract any non-magnetic object from the surface of the earth so that they might use this object in their studies."

La Razon asked the professor how parapsychology viewed such a theory. "From our viewpoint," Professor Eru answered, "we find it noteworthy that these beings can manage telepathy with such great mastery, because they seem to be able to make our minds understand things which cannot by expressed by speech. At the same time, they capture, without difficulty, our answers. Nothing more, with any seriousness, can be said of these phenomena at this time. But for some special reason, the North Americans have kept the Vidals' car in their powerful laboratories to examine it!" (Author's note: The Vidals' car, a Peugeot 403, was said to have been sent to the United States for examination in scientific laboratories. Dr. Vidal received another automobile of the same make in exchange for it.)

In the September-October, 1970, issue of *Flying Saucer Review*, Creighton reported that Mrs. Vidal died of leukemia early in 1969, "...this information having been revealed, through a slip, by a member of the family to an investigator whose country of origin is in continental Europe."

Could Mrs. Vidal's fatal bout with leukemia have been prompted by exposure to intense radiation during that bizarre forty-eight-hour disappearance and teleportation to Mexico?

And did the Vidals drive into a hole in Time and Space—a tear in our dimension which leads to another—or were they transported from one geographical location to another by beings from another world or another dimension?

In that same issue of *Flying Saucer Review*, Creighton reported several other alleged teleportations which occurred in South American countries shortly after the Vidals' mysterious flight.

A young newlywed Brazilian couple stopped for a rest as they traveled through the southern Brazilian state of Rio Grande do Sul. They were sitting in their Volkswagen when they were both overcome by drowsiness. When they awakened, they were in Mexico.

In another case in Rio Grande do Sul, two young men traveling by jeep claimed to have run into a bank of white fog. The next thing they knew was that they were on an unknown landscape which turned out to be in Mexico.

Creighton quotes the January 15, 1969, issue of the Rio de Janeiro newspaper, *Diario de Noticias*, which speaks of two other cases of instant transportation:

"There are rumors that two persons who were traveling in their car along the President Dutra Motorway were transported from there to a town in the USA and close to the Mexican border. The car bore marks made by the hooks of the transporting vehicle.

"Another Brazilian couple (named Azambuja) are also said to have been transported to Mexico in their car in similar circumstances."

It would seem that somewhere in Brazil there exists an ultradimensional shortcut to Mexico! Or were these automobiles really transported by some otherworldly, or other-dimensional vehicles?

In numerous cases discussed in other books, there have been reports of the simultaneous manifestation of mist, fog, or "white clouds" with the strange disappearances. Creighton recounts the experiences of Graciela del Lourdes Gimenez, an eleven-year-old Argentinian girl, who walked into a cloud of white mist and was not seen again for three hours. When she did reappear, she found herself in an unfamiliar section of town; weeping and in a distraught state, she appealed to a resident of the area for help.

In another instance, Senor Marcilo Ferraz and his wife encountered a white cloud on the road as they neared the frontier of Brazil and Uruguay. When they regained consciousness, they, too, found themselves in Mexico. Both of the Ferrazes suffered severe traumatic shock, and when Senor Ferraz learned that he had developed a tumor on the brain, he shot himself.

The newspapers *Diario de Noticias* and *Folha de Goias* both carried accounts of a bizarre case which occurred in the state of Goias, Brazil, on the night of April 20, 1969. In this instance, a Señor Dolor Roque saw some lights as he was riding into the town of Itacu on his horse to obtain some medicine from a pharmacy. When he next opened his eyes, he found himself on the bank of the Paranaiba River near a place known as Itumbiara—a distance of 250 miles from Itacu.

Hailing a man with a horse and a cart, Roque beseeched the driver to take him to the nearest bus station. When he returned to his home, he found his family very distressed by his disappearance, since the horse had made its way back to its stable the night before.

Researchers who set themselves the task of of investigating such baffling phenomena have long observed that those instances in which human beings, animals and such inanimate objects as stones, pottery, and buildings are transported from one place to another are among the most puzzling of all paranormal occurrences.

Author Harold T. Wilkins once commented that mysteries such as instances of teleportation "…should serve as a reminder that the physical universe holds surprises for those who rashly predetermine that all natural phenomena may be summed up in mathematical equations and neatly listed in a textbook. To scientists willing to consider the as yet unknown, teleportations stand as a challenge to research in a field no less real and potentially fruitful than atomic energy."

Wilkins has retold an account of an eerie case of an interrupted teleportation that occurred in Bristol, England, on December 9, 1873. In this instance an elderly couple who identified themselves as the Thomas Cumpstons told authorities an incredible story of being nearly sucked into a hole in space.

The Cumpstons had been staying at the Victoria Hotel across from the railroad station, preparatory to a visit to a seaside resort. At three that morning they had been awakened by a terrible noise in their room. The floor seemed to split and open, and their cries of terror seemed to be strangely repeated and re-echoed.

Thomas Cumpston fell down and began to vanish in the mysterious hole in the floor. Mrs. Cumpston got hold of her husband's arm and began to pull him to safety.

"We screamed," Mrs. Cumpston told the authorities, "yet each time our screams were most horribly re-echoed. I said to my husband, take out your pistol and fire it. He fired into the ceiling, yet the terrible noises continued."

In desperation, the couple fled by way of the bedroom window, dropping the ten feet to the street below them. They hurried to the railroad station where they told the night superintendent that they had escaped from a "den of thieves and rogues." Bristol police authorities searched the Cumpstons' hotel room but could find and nothing that could in any way account for the elderly couple's bizarre tale. When they interviewed the landlady, they obtained her comment that she had heard some strange noises coming from their room, but that the sounds were of a nature beyond her experience.

The Cumpstons were considered respectable people of good social position in their home city of Leeds, so they were dismissed in charge of their attorney and it was recorded in the official accounts that the couple had suffered a most remarkable kind of collective hallucination.

Harold T. Wilkins observed in his retelling of the strange tale that it becomes impossible to explain the strange noises and the hole in the floor "…unless one assumes that under certain conditions an unknown force operates which is able to create a vortex in solid matter. It should be noted that matter is 'solid' only relative to human perceptions; on the atomic level it may be described as mostly empty space. A human being drawn into such a vortex, or whirlpool…may be deposited in some spot dozens, and even thousands, of miles from his starting point…"

As we have already noted, things as well as people may be drawn into these weird vortexes and transported to other places or other dimensions. In 1968, an elderly Maine resident wrote a letter to the *Bangor Daily News* "On the Maine Street" column which told of a barn that totally disappeared during a rainstorm. According to Henry Davis, the incident occurred during the month of June, 1924. He remembered the day well because he had driven to the school to pick up his children so that they would not be drenched in the heavy rain.

About a mile out of the town of Monson, where the Davises lived at the time, there stood a large farm building known locally as "Sprague's Barn." The barn had been constructed of heavy, hand-sawn timbers and it stood in the midst of a large field. The next morning the residents of Monson were astonished to learn that the huge barn had completely disappeared. Although some people worked on the theory that a tornado had suddenly swooped down and picked up the large and sprawling building, the "twister" hypothesis seemed weak when it was noted that not a single shingle or bit of timber lay anywhere in the area. Letter-writer Davis went on to state that even though construction has been quite heavy in that area during the past sixty years, no one has ever found a single board, nail, or implement from "Sprague's Barn."

Frank Edwards, popular storyteller of the unusual, summarized an account of a vanishing Eskimo village for his book *Stranger than Science*. According to available records, the thirty inhabitants of the village on the shore of Lake Anjikuni had been going about their mundane daily tasks when they simply disappeared, leaving the Northwest Mounted Police with a most disturbing unsolved case on their hands.

Pots of food hung over dead fires. Ivory needles protruded from garments that were in the process of being mended. Kayaks lay battered and neglected at the lake's edge. Highly prized rifles stood beside the doorways of the empty huts. Seven dogs lay dead of starvation where they had been left tied to trees. And, perhaps most baffling of all, a fresh grave had been opened and the body had been removed.

In the Far North country, a man never leaves the camp on a journey of any consequence without taking his rifle with him. A dog is valued as highly as a fellow human being and is as much a part of a journey as is a rifle. As far as the empty grave is concerned, desecration of the dead is unthinkable to an Eskimo.

As Frank Edwards summarized the case: "Evidently the village of about thirty inhabitants had been pursuing its normal way of life when for some reason they rushed out of their huts and none of them ever got back from whatever had attracted their attention. For reasons unknown, the inhabitants of the village—men, women, and children—had left it, willingly or unwillingly, in the dead of early winter…. Skilled trackers failed to find any trail if they had fled over the tundra. The presence of their battered kayaks was mute evidence that they had not ventured out into the lake…. Months of patient and far-flung investigation failed to produce a single trace of any member who had lived in the deserted village of Anjikuni."

Volume thirty-two of the (British) *Journal of the Society for Psychical Research* carries statements from Mr. and Mrs. Clifford H. Pye in regard to a house that disappeared.

The Pyes were on a vacation trip, traveling by bus, when they sighted an attractive house on the outskirts of Boscastle on the coast of northern Cornwall.

According to Clifford Pye's statement, the bus had stopped to let off a passenger almost outside the gate of "…a rather substantial house standing on the left-hand side of the road. It stood back from the road some 20 yards or so… The house was double-fronted and of a style of architecture which I judged to date from the late 1860s or early 1870s. It had a fresh, trim appearance and seemed to have been recently painted..."

"The most striking feature, however, was on the lawn where amongst beds of scarlet geraniums there were several wicker or cane chairs or tables over which there were standing large garden umbrellas of black and orange."

Mr. and Mrs. Pye saw no one on the grounds and saw no sign identifying the place as a hotel, but they had no doubt that such was the case. Mrs. Pye expressed the sentiment that both of them shared. The place was just what they were looking for in a guest house for their stay in Boscastle.

But when the Pyes went back to the guest house to book rooms, they found "just empty fields running across the cliffs."

According to Clifford Pye: "During our stay...we made a thorough search of the locality, but failed to find .any place remotely resembling that we had seen. On a subsequent visit to the Travelga guest house I told our experience to the proprietor, who assured me that from his knowledge there was in the neighborhood no such house as I described."

Author Edmond P. Gibson, in referring to the case, wrote that the strange experience might best be explained as a collective hallucination "engendered by the Pyes' wish to find a suitable place for their vacation."

Although Gibson theorizes that one of the couple might have conjured the place up in the subconscious and the other might have viewed it telepathically, he admits that "...to call the incident a collective hallucination describes what occurred but does not explain it. There is no evidence that any such house ever stood on the site noted, so it cannot be called a ghost house, unless it was displaced in space. Yet there must have been some underlying cause in the subconscious minds of the Pyes that caused this vision to be seen at the same time by both."

Did the Pyes have a collective vision or did "some underlying cause" in their subconscious minds permit them a view of another dimension, another reality which sits somewhere on the edge of our own?

Mr. R. W. Balcom of Live Oak, California, contributed a personal experience shared with his wife to the September, 1968, issue of *Fate* magazine. According to Mr. Balcom, the two of them were traveling to Lake Tahoe during the early morning hours. A few miles east of Placerville on Highway 50, they stopped to eat at a quaint and rustic-styled restaurant, which neither of them had ever noticed on any of their previous trips to the region.

The food was excellent, and the waitress and cook were so friendly that the Balcoms truly meant their promise to stop back again.

They tried to do so on their return drive from Lake Tahoe, but the restaurant was nowhere to be seen. The Balcoms traveled that route three successive weekends in 1962, searching for the friendly little restaurant with the good food that had simply vanished into nothingness.

"Since then we have journeyed over Highway 50 to Lake Tahoe many times," Balcom concludes, "never again finding the little restaurant."

Did the Balcoms have the same kind of collective hallucination that the Clifford Pyes shared? Or were both couples subconsciously tuned to enter the higher, or lower, vibratory rate of another dimension?

Lois B. Tracy told of the night in 1934 when she was driving with her family on a stretch of road between Bartow and Ft. Meade, Florida, when the Model T Ford in front of them drifted sideways off the road and into the swamp and disappeared. "My father jammed on the brakes. We could not understand what happened," she writes (*Fate*, June 1964). "The car had not driven off the road, but just had drifted sideways. We pointed our headlights into the swamp and we looked with flashlights, but we could find no sign of that car."

Frances E. Peterson of Keokuk, Iowa, remembered the Sunday afternoon in 1935, when she, her husband, and their four children were returning from a weekend visit in Missouri. They decided to take a shortcut on a dirt road. They drove down a hill into a valley, then as they reached the rim of the valley, they were astonished to see "…a well where women in sun bonnets and long, full skirts covered by large aprons were drawing in a wooden pail by a windlass. Other women were carrying the water in pails balanced on wooden yokes across their shoulders. Bearded men, who were tending sheep and gathering wood, wore loose-fitting trousers, smocks, and large black hats."

The Petersons had never heard of such a settlement in the area of St. Patrick, Missouri, and as it turned out, no one else had either.

"Many times since then we have looked for this lovely Old World settlement," Mrs. Peterson commented. "We have inquired of old settlers and relatives in the area...but no one knows of such a valley....Did we ride backward in time?" (*Fate*, April 1959)

The men and women who have had the experiences cited above will always wonder whether or not they had some kind of collective psychic experience or whether their physical bodies somehow managed to pass into another dimension. For other individuals the answer becomes a bit more clearly stated, although no more clearly defined or explained, for they were left with undeniable physical evidence that they had been confronted with some force as yet beyond the grasp of orthodox science.

At about 2:00 P.M. on Tuesday, April 17, 1951, Mrs. Ernest Harrleson was working in her farm home south of Georgetown, South Carolina, when she heard a peculiar sound overhead. She had had no time to puzzle out the sound before it was climaxed with a loud ripping sound.

Mrs. Harrleson dashed out her front door to see a shower of shingles and bits of lumber dropping out of the sky. More than half the roof had been torn off an unoccupied tenant house across the road and a bit west of the Harrleson home.

Walter S. McDonald, writing in the Charleston, South Carolina, *News and Courier* for April 24, 1951, stated: "The single section of the roof which did not fall to the rear lies to the right and front of the house, some 50 feet away, while the remainder is scattered over an area of about 150 by 100 feet at the back. There were no signs of burns and the floor was undamaged except where the chimney fell through. There were many tin and wood shingles scattered about individually, but some small sections of the roof were included in the debris. Small timbers of the roof were broken apart cleanly, as if snapped in half by a powerful force."

Yet no one could identify that "powerful force" Roofs of buildings, barns, unfortunate men, women, and children may have been claimed by some as yet unidentified "force," or these people and things may have been somehow translated into another dimension.

the horrible hag
of detroit

When the William Adams family moved into the gray frame house on Martin Street in Detroit, Michigan, only the children and the dog seemed to sense that something loathsome had made its abode in the back bedroom.

There was certainly nothing about the physical appearance of the room that made Adams and his wife Lillian suspect that the small bedroom could hold a thing of unspeakable terror. For one thing, it was such a tiny room. There was only space enough in the minis-cule enclosure for a bed and a built-in closet in one corner. Because it was so small and so far removed from the rest of the house, Adams used to sleep in it when he came home from the midnight shift at the Cadillac plant.

"Even after years of working the midnight shift," Adams explained, "I still have trouble, sometimes, sleeping in the daytime."

It was not long before Adams noticed the strange and uncom-fortable effect that the back bedroom seemed to have on him. "I started having the most horrible nightmares you can imagine," he said later to a reporter from the *Detroit Free Press*. "They would leave me limp with fear because they were so real. I would find myself sitting in the bed screaming until my throat was sore.

"One of the dreams was when I found myself opening a door and a mutilated body fell out."

The ghastly nightmares began to rob Adams of so much sleep that he told his wife, "If this doesn't stop, I don't know what I'll do. I'm about ready to see a psychiatrist."

It was only after he had resumed sleeping in the master bedroom that he began to associate the nightmares with the back bedroom. "I didn't have any bad dreams when I slept in our bedroom. The nightmares would come only when I slept in that terrible room."

In August of 1962, Adams' grandmother came to visit them from Georgia. Both the Adamses assumed that Bill's reaction to the room had been some kind of personal association, so they gave Grandmother Adams the back bedroom for use during her stay.

The next morning she came to the breakfast table pale and shaken. "There are terrible sounds in that room," she told them. "All night long I thought someone was trying to break in. I refuse to sleep in that room again."

Grandmother Adams became so uneasy in the house that she cut short her stay and returned to Georgia.

For the first time, Bill and Lillian began to realize that there was something terrible about that room. They began to recall things— small things that had seemed inconsequential at the time. They remembered, for example, that their small terrier refused to enter the room, that eight-year-old Jimmy, six-year-old Deborah, five-year-old Johnny, two-year-old Laurie, and the baby, Tammy, always avoided the room when they played about the house. What strange thing was tainting the atmosphere in that tiny back bedroom?

On October 27th, an old friend from Georgia, Shirley Patterson, arrived to spend a few days with the Adamses in Detroit before he drove a new car back home to Decatur. Adams knew that Patterson was a practical, matter-of-fact Southerner. Bill and Lillian decided he would be their final test. If Patterson could spend a night in the back bedroom without suffering any ill effects or reporting anything strange, perhaps they had merely let their imaginations gain the upper hand. They would not even mention their own unpleasant experiences with the room. Patterson would be able to explode all the fantasies that they had built up about the room.

"I didn't know anything about the room," Patterson said later. "There was no reason for me to suspect anything. No reason to be afraid.

"It seems that I was in the bed for just a few minutes. I don't know whether I was asleep or not. I was facing the wall, and then I felt something turn me over. Don't ask me to describe the feeling. All I know is that it rolled me over and then I saw it standing outside the bedroom door.

"At first I thought it was Lillian, but I started to tremble. It was a woman with long hair, and she had her back to me looking into the kitchen. She was wearing a short fur coat and a kind of blue dress."

Patterson screamed as loud as he could and ran toward the figure. At the moment he approached it, every light in the house went out.

He continued to stumble around in the darkness until, a moment later, the lights came back on again. He met Lillian in the kitchen. Bill had left shortly before for the midnight shift at the plant.

"In the bedroom" Patterson began, "I saw…"

His words of explanation were suddenly interrupted by a terrible wailing—a mournful half-human, half-animal sound that left both of them speechless with fright.

"It was like nothing I'd ever heard before," Lillian Adams recalled later, "and then there was an awful smell that made both of us sick. It was coming from the room where we heard the moaning."

As if the unearthly moaning and the nauseating stench were not enough, a heavy trapdoor in the floor of the utility room raised itself several inches into the air and then fell back into place again. Below the trapdoor was a set of flimsy stairs that led to a partially dug-out basement.

Freeing themselves at last from the spell of terror that had completely engulfed them, the frightened man and woman called the police. Within a few minutes, officers were searching the house from attic to incompleted basement. They were able to find nothing that would give a rational explanation to the apparition which Patterson had seen or to the eerie moaning and the sickening odor, which both Patterson and Lillian Adams had noted.

When Adams got home from the plant on Sunday morning, October 28th, his wife and friend were waiting up for him. As calmly as they could they told him what they had experienced that night.

"I'm not the kind of guy who believes in ghosts—at least I didn't then," Adams said. "I'm a grown man with a family. I've been in the Army. I just couldn't convince myself that there was anything to it. I had to try again and see what would happen."

That night, at about 7:30 P.M., Adams lay down on the bed in the back bedroom. He had reached a decision that night, once and for all; he would either conquer whatever inhabited the room or he would admit defeat and let the thing have the bedroom—and the house—to itself.

He had lain in the bedroom for quite some time when he thought he heard Lillian moving in the room. He had left his friend and his wife sitting silently in the front room with a small table lamp providing their only light.

"Lil," Adams whispered sharply, "you'd better leave the room if we're ever going to get anything settled. It probably won't show itself if there's two of us in here."

There was no answer and no sound of movement, but Adams still sensed a presence in the room.

"I turned over to look and the face was inches away from me. It was the most horrible thing I have ever seen. The eyes stared past me and the mouth moved to talk but only a hissing noise came out—and a terrible stench!"

Adams ran out of the back bedroom in a state of near hysteria. He was screaming wildly, and he ripped handfuls of hair from his head as he ran into the kitchen. Patterson tried to grab him and hold him down, but Adams flailed away at his friend as if he were berserk. Finally Lillian and Patterson managed to throw a blanket over Bill and wrestle him to the floor. The same nauseating stench they had noticed the night before once again permeated the house.

An hour after Bill had regained his senses and told of the ghastly and indescribably evil face he had seen, the house on Martin

Street was empty. Adams had admitted defeat. The horrid hag could keep her bedroom and her house. They grabbed the sleeping children from their beds and fled in the night to neighbors. The next morning they moved in with Mrs. Adams' parents, who live in Dearborn, a suburb of Detroit.

"All I could think of that next morning," Adams remarked, "was that if the bedroom door had been closed that Sunday night, I would have killed myself beating against it to get out."

With the help of friends and relatives, the Adamses found another house to rent and moved all of their furniture out of the house on Martin Street during a series of daylight visits.

Mrs. Adams' brother, Leo Sanocki, and her sister Virginia arrived at the house one night to see for themselves if there was anything to Lillian's and Bill's wild tale of an ugly hag that haunted the back bedroom.

"I stood out in the kitchen and Leo said he was going to lie down on the bed for ten minutes in the dark," said Virginia Sanocki. "A few minutes later I heard this awful groan come from the back bedroom. If it was Leo, I have never heard him make a sound like that before.

"Then he came rushing through the door into the kitchen with the most horrible look on his face, like he was scared out of his mind. I asked him what he saw, but he wouldn't tell me anything."

Leo Sanocki refused to disclose what he had seen in that back bedroom in the house on Martin Street in Detroit. And, as the landlady absolutely refused to let any investigators into the house with any electronic equipment, it is unlikely that we shall ever know what mission kept the horrible hag haunting that bedroom in Detroit.

the poltergeist that killed

lthough physical violence toward a certain member of the family is characteristic of several poltergeist cases, I am aware of only one recorded instance where the poltergeist was actually responsible for murder. On December 19, 1820, John Bell was poisoned by the "witch" that had inhabited their home for four years.

The disturbances began with mysterious rappings on the windows of the Bell's cabin near Clarksville, Tennessee. Elizabeth Bell began to complain of an invisible "rat" gnawing on her bedpost at night. The entire family experienced the midnight confusion of having their covers pulled off their beds. Everyone heard a strange sucking noise, an eerie smacking of lips, as if an invisible baby were being nursed.

Several investigators of poltergeist phenomena have noted these same peculiar sounds of psychic "nursing." Some researchers have noted that these "signal" noises often occur shortly before an evening of particularly violent disturbances. It is as if the poltergeist is some kind of obscene infant being "born" of projected frustrations and repressions. Sacheverell Sitwell wrote of the "birth" of a poltergeist in this manner: "It babbles, as though in the struggles of life or death. It is dying, or but just born, an embryonic phantasm which is only upon the borderlands, upon one frontier or the other, of human life. None can pity it or feel sorrow for it. There is an obscene or drivelling sense to it.... It is in all things unholy, unhallowed, and not human. Who can doubt that it is the projection, not of the brain, but of the obscene senses, of the deep, hidden underworld which is at the back of every mind."

When the Bell family arose one morning, stones littered the floor of their front room and the furniture had been overturned. The children, Elizabeth, John, Drewry, Joel, and Richard were goggle-eyed and spoke of ghosts and goblins. John Bell lectured his family severely: "We shall keep this problem to ourselves. We don't want our family to become the subject for common and unsavory gossip."

That night, Richard was awakened by something pulling his hair, raising his head right off the pillow. Joel began screaming at his brother's plight, and from her room, Elizabeth began howling that the gnawing rat had begun to pull her hair, too.

Most of the family awakened the next day with sore scalps, and John reversed his decision. It was obvious that the Bell family needed help. That day he would confide in James Johnson, their nearest neighbor and closest friend.

Johnson accompanied his friend to the cabin that evening. The tale that Bell told was an incredible one, but Johnson knew that his neighbor was not given to flights of fancy. While he watched at Elizabeth's bedside that night, Johnson saw the young girl receive several blows on the cheeks from an invisible antagonist.

"Stop in the name of the Lord Jesus Christ!" Johnson adjured the phantom assailant.

There was no activity from the poltergeist for several minutes, then Betsy's hair received a yank that brought a cry of pain from her lips. Again Johnson adjured the "evil spirit" and it released the girl's hair.

"I conclude that the spirit understands the human language," Johnson told Bell. The wise Mr. Johnson was also able to determine that Betsy was the center of the haunting. He met with other neighbors, and they decided to help the Bell family as best they could.

First a committee decided to keep watch at the Bell house all night to try to placate the spirit. All this accomplished was to bring about an especially vicious attack on the unfortunate Betsy. A number of neighbors volunteered their own daughters to sleep with the girl, but this only managed to terrorize the other girls as well. Nor did it accomplish any useful purpose to take Betsy out of the cabin into the home of neighbors—the trouble simply followed her there and upset the entire house.

By now the haunting had achieved wide notoriety, and the disturbances were thought to be the work of a witch, who had set her evil spirits upon the Bell family. Each night the house was filled with those who sat up trying to get the "witch" to talk or to communicate with them by rapping on the walls or by smacking its lips. There seems little doubt that somehow the phenomenon was able to "feed" itself upon the psyches of these "true believers."

The disturbances soon became powerful enough to venture outside the cabin and away from Betsy, its center of energy. Neighbors reported seeing lights "like candles or lamps" flitting through the fields, and farmers began to suffer stone-throwing attacks from the Bell Witch.

These particular peltings seemed to have been more in the nature of fun than some of the other manifestations of the poltergeist. Young boys in the area would often play catch with the Witch if she happened to throw something at them on their way home from school. Once an observer witnessed several boys get suddenly pelted with sticks that flew from a nearby thicket. The sticks did not strike the boys with much force, and, with a great deal of laughter, the boys scooped the sticks up and hurled them back into the thicket.

Once again, the sticks came flying back out. The observer cut notches in several of the sticks with his knife before the boys once again returned the Witch's volley. He was able to identify his markings when the playful poltergeist once again flung the sticks from the thicket.

The Witch was not so gentle with the scoffers who had come to the Bell home to "expose the manifestations as trickery." Those who stayed the night invariably had their covers jerked from their beds. If they resisted the Witch's yanking, they were slapped soundly on the face. "The blows were heard distinctly," one of the family noted in a diary, "like the open palm of a hand..."

Spiritists, clergymen, reporters, and curiosity seekers had waged a ceaseless campaign that sought to urge the Witch to talk and declare herself and her intentions. At last their efforts were rewarded. At first the voice was only a whistling kind of indistinct babble, then it became bolder —a husky whisper speaking from darkened corners. At last, it became a full-toned voice that spoke not only in darkness but also in lighted rooms and finally, during the day as well as the night.

Immediately the charge of ventriloquism was heard from the skeptical. To put a halt to the accusations of trickery, John Jr. brought in a doctor, who placed his hand over Betsy's mouth and listened at her throat while the Witch's voice chattered amicably from a far corner of the room. The doctor decreed that the girl was "in no way connected with these sounds." A modern day psychical researcher would have qualified that statement adding, "at least not by ventriloquism." Twelve-year old Betsy Bell had begun to suffer from seizures and fainting spells very similar to those which mediums undergo before entering into trance. Observers noted that spells came on at regular hours, just before the Witch put in an appearance. After Betsy recovered, the Witch would begin to speak. The Witch was always silent while the girl lay prostrate upon her bed.

From the very beginning of the Witch's visitation, it had minced no words in its dislike of John Bell, Betsy's father. "I'll keep after him until the end of his days," the Witch often swore to visitors in the Bell home. "Old Jack Bell's days are numbered."

Even before the Witch had begun to manifest itself by the rapping on the windows and the hair-pulling, John Bell had complained of a strange pain in his throat. He described it as feeling like "a stick stuck crosswise punching each side of my jaws." As the phenomenon progressed, Bell was often plagued by a tongue that swelled against his mouth, so that "he could neither talk nor eat for ten or fifteen hours."

It has been suggested that the onset of John Bell's physical afflictions and his daughter's psychic persecution was no coincidence. Dr. Nandor Fodor, writing of the Bell Witch, makes the observation that the swelling of Bell's tongue suggests that he may have been keeping a dreadful secret that sought physical release. Dr. Fodor also speculates that Betsy, approaching puberty, may have undergone a shocking sexual experience for which her father was responsible. "It was probably to save her reason," Dr. Fodor wrote, "that a fragment of her mind was split off and became the Bell Witch." If this theory is true, it may account for the remarkable range and power of the Bell poltergeist. Psychically, the phenomenon was being fed by sexual shock, pubertal change and a father's guilt. To a visitor's question concerning its identity, the Witch once answered: "I am a spirit who was once very happy, but who has been disturbed and made made unhappy. I will remain in this house and worry old Jack Bell until I kill him."

Later, the Witch declared itself to be the spirit of an Indian and sent the family on a wild "bone chase" to gather up all of its skeletal remains. "If my bones are all put back together, I'll be able to rest in peace," the poltergeist lied to them.

"I'm really the ghost of old Kate Batts," the Witch told the family with a merry cackle as they confessed their inability to find all of the Indian's bones. Kate Batts had been an eccentric recluse who had earned the appellation of "witch" from the citizens of Clarksville. When the word spread that it was the ghost of old Kate Batts who was haunting the Bells, the entire mystery became much more believable to several doubting neighbors.

The Bell home became crowded, indeed, when the Witch's "family" moved in with her. Four hell-raisers named Blackdog, Mathematics, Cypocryphy, and Jerusalem, each speaking in distinct voices of their own, made every night a party night during their stay with their "mother." The sounds of raucous laughter rattled the shingles of the Bell home, and witnesses noted the strong scent of whiskey that permeated every room in the house.

When two local preachers arrived to investigate the disturbances, the Witch delivered each of their Sunday sermons word for word and in a perfect imitation of their own voices.

The Bell Witch was, as are all poltergeists, adept at producing odd objects apparently from thin air. Once, at one of Mrs. Bell's Bible study groups, the ladies were showered with fresh fruits. Betsy's friends were treated to bananas at one of her birthday parties. "Those came from the West Indies," the Witch told the delighted girls. "I picked them myself."

Although the father, John Bell, was the butt of malicious pranks and cruel blows, Mrs. Bell was looked after solicitously by the Witch. Once when Mrs. Bell was ill, the Witch was heard to say: "Poor Luce. Hold out your hands, I have something for you."

Mrs. Bell held out her hands and a large quantity of hazelnuts dropped into her palms. "Eat them," the Witch instructed her." They will do you good."

"But I cannot crack them," Mrs. Bell said weakly.

"Then I shall do it for you," the Witch answered. Family and neighbors watched in wide-eyed fascination as the nuts cracked open and the meats were sorted from the shells.

Next to the materialization of fruits and nuts, the Witch was especially fond of producing pins and needles. Mrs. Bell was provided with enough pins to supply the entire county, but sometimes the Witch would impishly hide them in the bedclothes or in chair cushions—points out.

John Jr., Betsy's favorite brother, was the only member of the family besides the mother who received decent treatment from the Witch. Joel and Richard were often whipped soundly by the invisible force, and Drewry was so frightened of the Witch that he never married, fearing that the entity might someday return and single out his own family for particular attention. John Jr. was the only one of Betsy's brothers who could "sass back" at the Witch and get away with it. The Witch even went to special pains to get John Jr. to like it, and the mysterious entity often performed demonstrations of ability solely for his benefit.

Elizabeth and her father, of course, received the brunt of the Witch's ill nature. The cruelest act perpetrated on Betsy was the breaking of her engagement to Josh Gardner. The two young people were acclaimed by friends to be "ideally suited for one another," but the Witch protested violently when the engagement was announced.

"She will never know a day of happiness if she marries Joshua," the Witch told John Jr. "You must aid me in preventing the union."

The Witch screamed at Joshua whenever he entered the Bell home and embarrassed both young people by shouting obscenities about them in front of their friends. Richard Bell noted in his diary that the "vile devil—never ceased to practice upon her fears, insult her modesty, stick pins in her body, pinching and bruising her flesh, slapping her cheeks, dishevelling and tangling her hair, tormenting her in many ways until she surrendered that most cherished hope which animates every young heart."

A friend of the family, Frank Miles, learned of the Witch's objection to Betsy's engagement and resolve to stand up to the "evil spirit" on her behalf. As an elderly woman in her eighties, Elizabeth remembered how Miles "fairly shook the house, stamping on the floor, swearing terribly."

"Take any form you so desire," Miles threatened, "and I'll take you on." He made motions in the air as if warming up for a wrestling match. "Just let me get a hold of you, and we'll soon send you packing. I'm not afraid of an invisible windbag." Suddenly Miles' head jerked backwards as if a solid slap had stung his cheeks. He put up his forearms to block a series of facial blows, then dropped his guard as he received a serious punch in the stomach. Mill slumped against a wall, desperately shaking his head to recover his senses.

"Begone," he heard the Witch's voice warn him, "or I'll knock your block off!"

Frank Miles looked helplessly at Betsy Bell, who had watched the one-sided boxing match. Reluctantly, he picked up his hat and coat. A man couldn't fight an enemy he couldn't see. With the decisive defeat of her champion, Betsy had no choice but to give in to the Witch's demands and break her engagement with Joshua Gardner. On the night in which Betsy returned the ring, the Witch's laughter could be heard ringing victoriously from every room in the house

Shortly after the entity had accomplished the severing of Betsy's marriage agreement with her fiancée, it once more began to concentrate its energy on the destruction of John Bell. Richard was walking with his father on that day in December of 1820 when John Bell collapsed into a spasmodically convulsing heap. Young Richard was terrified by the agonies that beset his wretched father and wrote later that his facial contortions were so hideous that they seemed to "convert him into a very demon to swallow me up."

John Bell was brought home to his bed where he lay for several days in a very weakened condition. Even during the man's illness, the Witch would not leave him in peace, but continued to torment him by slapping his face and throwing his legs into the air. On the morning of December 19, 1820, John Bell lapsed into a stupor from which he would never be aroused. John Jr. went quickly to the medicine cabinet to obtain his father's prescription and found instead "a smoky looking vial, which was about one-third full of dark colored liquid."

"It's no use to try to revive Old Jack," the Witch cackled. "I've got him at last."

"Where did this vial come from?" John Jr. demanded of the voice.

"I put it there last night," the Witch answered smugly. "I gave Old Jack a big dose of it while he was asleep. I fixed him!"

John Jr. sent for the doctor. When the physician arrived, he asked one of the boys to fetch a cat from the barn. While John Jr. held the cat, the doctor dipped a straw into the dark vial and wiped it on the animal's tongue. The cat jumped into the air, whirled about on the floor, and "died very quick."

The Witch sang bawdy songs all during John Bell's funeral and annoyed the assembled mourners with the sounds of its crude celebration throughout the man's last rites.

After the death of Betsy's father, the Witch behaved much better toward the young woman. It never again inflicted pain upon her and actually addressed her in terms of endearment. The psychic energy which nurtured the poltergeist seemed to be waning. During the rest of the winter and on into the spring months, the manifestations decreased steadily. Then, one night after the evening meal, a large smoke ball seemed to roll down from the chimney of the fireplace out into the room. As it burst, a voice told the family: "I'm going now, and I will be gone for seven years."

True to its word, the Witch returned to the homestead in 1828. Betsy had entered into a successful marriage with another man; John Jr. had married and now farmed land of his own. Only Mrs. Bell, Joel, and Richard remained on the home place. The disturbances consisted of the Witch's most elementary pranks—rappings, scratchings, pulling the covers off the bed—and the family agreed to ignore the unwanted guest. Their psychology worked, and the Witch left them after two weeks of pestering them for attention. The entity sought out John Jr. and told him in a fit of pique that it would return to one of his descendants in "one hundred years and seven."

Dr. Charles Bailey Bell should have been the recipient of the Bell Witch's unwelcome return visit, but Dr. Bell and his family survived the year 1935 without hearing the slightest unexplained scratch or undetermined rapping. Dr. Bell has written the official record of the mysterious disturbances endured by his ancestors in *The Bell Witch. A Mysterious Spirit.*

Dr. Bell notes the precognitive powers of the Witch in a series of "wonderful things" and prophecies which the entity revealed to his grandfather, John Bell, Jr. The Witch predicted the Civil War, the emancipation of the Negroes, the acceleration of the United States as a world power, the two world wars (the date for World War II was off by only four years), and the destruction of our civilization by "rapidly expanding heat, followed by a mighty explosion." Thankfully, this last prediction is not dated.

the thing
in the bloody,
haunted basement

pril 20, 1970. I held the negatives up to the light, squinted as my
eyes focused on the strange, reversed sight. "Yes" I said into the
receiver. "I can see it. It looks like a baby's face on the basement wall."

Dick Mezzy's voice crackled at me over the long-distance
wire. "That's exactly what it is, Brad. I'm not going to give you
any more details about the place now, but I hope that those negatives will intrigue you enough to direct your psychic safari to Lincoln for a few days."

Dick, who was at that time associated with the *Lincoln Journal and
Star*, had become a local authority on the occult, the paranormal, and
the UFO phenomenon in his corner of Nebraska. An exuberant and
talented young man, who was, incidentally, developing rather impressive psychic abilities of his own, Mezzy had become the Nebraska
clearing house for reports of unidentified flying objects, haunted
houses, and things that go bump in the night. Since he had done some
preliminary research on the house in question, which we shall call the

Richard house, I knew that a recommendation from Dick Mezzy was an assurance that the home offered a number of psychic surprises.

Our safari checked into the Holiday Inn on the east edge of Lincoln about two o'clock on a blisteringly hot July afternoon. Glenn McWane called Dick and let him know that we had arrived. Mezzy told Glenn that he had confirmed our tour of the house with Mrs. Richard for that night.

"We'll have to be out of there before ten, though," Mezzy said. "That's when her husband will be coming home from his shift, and he would blow all gaskets if he found us there. He doesn't want anyone stirring up what is already there."

Glenn told the newsman that we quite understood the situation, as it was not an uncommon condition under which, from time to time, we were forced to carry out our ghost hunting.

Dick joined us for dinner that night, then left his sports car at the motel in order to commandeer my station wagon and drive us to the Richard's home.

"Now I've purposely not told you anything about the place," Dick said somewhat apologetically to Irene Hughes. "I hope I understood that that was the way you wanted it."

"That's exactly the way we want it," Irene replied. "I want to be totally free of any preconceived ideas or thoughts before I enter any of the houses on our psychic safari."

"Well, good, then," Mezzy said as we rounded a corner and began to slow down. "Here's the house. Sic 'em, Irene!"

It was late twilight, and the air had not yet cooled from the day's extremely high temperatures. The Richard house seemed to crouch there before us like some panting beast, worn and tired from the summer heat. Although it was obviously an old house, it did not appear quite as ominous as some of the houses which we had visited on our safari. There was, though, a strange kind of presence, or vibration, that I think most of us seemed to feel as we walked through the screen door to be received by Mrs. Richard.

"Sorry we don't have air conditioning," Mrs. Richard apologized. "Terrible hot night. We have a lot of these in Nebraska."

We hastened to assure her that we were all Midwesterners and were as accustomed to heat and humidity as anyone could ever get.

Mrs. Richard was obviously very nervous, and when Mezzy introduced her to Mrs. Hughes, the woman seemed to be torn between a desire to curtsy and a desire to run screaming from the house.

Melody, her daughter, blinked large, frightened fawn eyes at us, and acknowledged our greetings in soft, unintelligible mumbles. A slender girl in her mid-teens, Melody seemed at once eager to get on with things, yet visibly concerned over what might materialize.

"That lady's a psychic," I heard her tell a girlfriend. "She's gonna make that awful ghost go away."

"Most of the things have happened in the basement, isn't that right?" Mezzy said, sensing the need for a direction to the evening. I appreciated his assuming the role of guide in the Richard house, since he had met the woman and her daughter previously and had even counseled with them about the phenomena that had continued to feed and grow in the environment of their home.

"Yes," Mrs. Richard admitted. "But we don't have to go down there, do we?"

"It would be better if we could be in the area where you have experienced the most disturbances," I explained.

The mother and daughter exchanged quick, worried glances. "If we take these people down there and they stir up the haunting even more than it was before, what will become of us?" It appeared as though they might be saying to each other. "It is well and good for these strangers. They will leave. But we have to stay here and suffer the consequences!"

"I won't go down there even in the daytime unless...unless I have someone with me," Mrs. Richard said softly, as if she were concerned about someone overhearing her admission.

"We'll all be with you now," Irene said in her soft, soothing voice. "You have nothing to be afraid of. And we won't set anything loose on you before we leave."

The daughter emitted a strange little whimpering sound. Dick Mezzy stepped to her side and whispered something to her.

Since I had had time to pay closer attention to Melody, it appeared as if she might nearly be in an altered state of consciousness, as though she were about to enter trance. Although I could not overhear Dick's conversation with the teenager, he seemed to be speaking to her in a kind of gruff, big brother fashion, which was totally applicable to the situation. I knew that I was making an extremely superficial assessment, but it seemed to me that Melody tottered somewhere in a borderland of reality that could lead to hysteria, involuntary mediumship, or temporary possession.

"The door to the basement is back through the living room and kitchen," Mrs. Richard said, at last making up her mind to permit us access to what was ostensibly the seat of the haunting. Following her resolve, she even led the way down the stairs and into a back room of the damp, cluttered basement.

"Who draws the paintings on the wall?" Irene asked, indicating the bright artwork that littered the floor, and in some instances had been applied directly to the wall.

"I do," Melody said, apparently quite proud of her artistic ability. Irene turned back to the wall, then caught her breath in a sharp intake of air that became a startled gasp.

"What is it?" a number of us chorused in unison, at once solicitous of the medium's welfare and curious to know what she had glimpsed with the aid of her psychism.

"I saw the image of a man coming through that wall!" Irene said. "His hair was long and unkempt. He was unshaven with a thick beard."

Melody's eyes widened, and she once again uttered that strange kind of panting whimper. "I've seen him before. I've seen him before when I've been down here painting!"

"He has a very thin face, and his hair is very shaggy," Irene said. "I had the impression that he was a wanderer. That he was unsettled. I felt as though he wanted to come home and he considered this his home."

"I know who he is, too!" Melody said loudly. "He's that man who used to live here who blew his wife's head off with a shotgun!"

Dick Mezzy rolled his eyes upward in disappointment and controlled anger. "Melody," he said through gritted teeth, "I asked you to give Mrs. Hughes any clues as to what's happened here!"

"But I've seen that man she's described coming at me out from the wall!" Melody protested in a loud voice, as if repetition and increased volume could vindicate her blunder.

"It's all right," Irene said. "Don't feel bad." Then, turning to Mrs. Richard, the psychic asked frankly: "You've seen him, too, haven't you?"

"Yes," the woman answered. Her face had grown pale and her hands trembled, as she touched a handkerchief to the beads of sweat on her forehead. "Yes, I've seen something very similar to what you describe."

"I saw him coming through the wall over there," Irene said, pointing to a back wall of the small room off the main basement area. "Do you feel that somebody might have died in this room? Do you feel that a man may have been stabbed to death?"

Mrs. Richard watched the back wall as if she feared that the ghost might appear at any moment. "You...you go ahead with your talking," she said, declining to answer the question Mrs. Hughes had posed for her.

"I see a man who I feel was stabbed and it looks like his heart is stabbed and cut. It looks like someone had carved a cross over his heart," the psychic said.

"There is a theory that a man, a murder victim may have been found in that condition in this house," Mezzy said. "I can't find any proof of that. However, it does seem to be neighborhood legend—along with that shotgun murder—which did happen."

Irene turned to focus her attention on Melody. "You have sometimes been able to see the blood running from the wall."

"Yes!" the girl agreed. "Yes!"

"And you," Irene said, readdressing herself to the mother. "Didn't you once turn on a tap in the basement to do your washing and see blood running out of the faucet?"

Mrs. Richard looked very much as if she wanted desperately to leave the basement. "Yes," she admitted. "I have just completely stopped using the basement."

"You turned on the spout and it looked like blood coming out of the faucet," Irene repeated.

Mrs. Richard nodded. "That's one of the reasons why I simply will not go down in the basement alone even in the daylight. I won't come down here anytime unless someone comes with me."

"And there is the form of a woman who bothers you," Irene said, zeroing in on the phenomena. "She is a fussy, argumentative woman who constantly talks and nags, and you wish that you could tell her to shut up!"

"I have told her," Mrs. Richard said, "but it hasn't seemed to do any good."

"Did you, about a week or two ago, awaken because there was a man shaking you and telling you to wake up?" Mrs. Hughes asked.

Mrs. Richard nodded. "Yes, I did. That's true."

"You awakened to see a man bending over you," Mrs. Hughes continued. "You knew at once that he was in spirit."

"But I didn't know *who* it was!" Mrs. Richard protested.

Mrs. Hughes stood for a few moments in silence. "I have the feeling that it was your father's brother. I see that the initial 'D' would belong to that man."

"That's right," Mrs. Richard said. "I mean, if it was my uncle, his name began with a 'D.' "

"That next morning you got up and folded some bedclothes and old blankets, and you put them in a box," Irene told the woman. "You put them away because they reminded you of something and someone in your past, and you just didn't want to bother with them anymore. Is that right?"

Mrs. Richard nodded her head slowly, unbelievingly. "That's right, I did that."

Irene Hughes turned her attention back to the mysterious little room in which most of our party now stood.

"This is funny," she mused, "but up on that ledge I see what looks like the shell of something. I thought at first it looked like it might have been a watermelon. Was it a large gourd?"

"It was my pumpkin!" Melody volunteered. "I carved a jack-o'-lantern and put it on that ledge. And it just disappeared. I mean, it vanished. I never saw it again, and none of us could find it anywhere."

Irene considered this information for a moment. "A similar thing happened to a pair of your blue jeans, isn't that right, Melody? You were looking everywhere for these jeans, and when you found them, they were wadded up under your bed."

Melody nodded soberly. "That happens to me a lot," she said.

An excellent example of a haunted house! This was the home of Native Americans on a reservation in Maine. The image in the lower-left window does not result from a photo flash or any other explainable cause. Photo: Ed & Lorraine Warren

The terrible basement in Lincoln, Nebraska. From left to right: Brad Steiger, journalist Dick Mezzy, and Irene Hughes. See "The Thing in the Bloody, Haunted Basement," p. 109.

Irene Hughes points out an area of psychic disturbance where an eerie white ghost dog had been frequently sighted.

Irene Hughes, noted seer and psychic investigator from Chicago.

Irene Hughes and a journalist enter another haunted basement, this one in Iowa.

On psychic safari—approaching a house in Illinois reported to be haunted. From left to right, Brad Steiger, Irene Hughes, and Glenn McWane.

Spontaneously manifesting handwriting from Borley Rectory, "the most haunted house in England." See "The Vicious Devil of Borley," p. 21. This actual specimen was bequeathed to Steiger by one of the investigators of the remarkable phenomena.

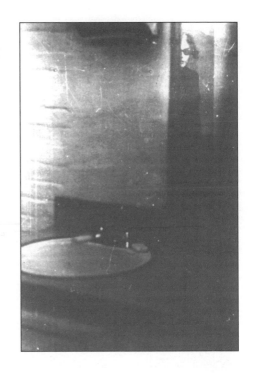

Ghost of the unfaithful mistress of a Russian embassy staff member manifesting in the mirror of the women's restroom of the embassy.

Alene Graham, left, wife of one of Brad Steiger's research associates, with a woman who claimed she could not be photographed. Even though other pictures on the same roll of film turned out perfectly, and although the woman has been photographed many times by a variety of people, she was right: she never shows up on film! See the account of a similar case in "Men and Women Who Walk Through Doorways to Other Dimensions," page 65.

The Steiger family (circa 1973) in front of their haunted farmhouse in Iowa. See story on page 55.

Kitchen entrance to the Steiger haunted farmhouse in Iowa.

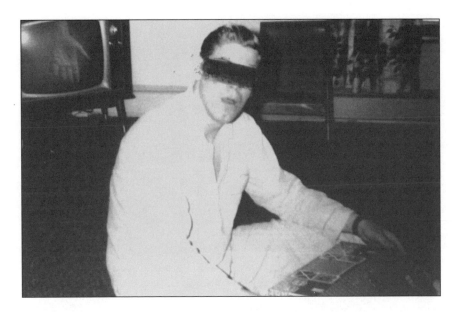

This photo was taken on Christmas Eve of 1968 in southern Minnesota. The man is assembling toys and is unaware of the mysterious hand manifesting on the unplugged television set! The outstretched hand appeared during two consecutive Christmas seasons.

This photo—not a double exposure—shows a ghostly image unscrewing a light bulb in a home near Lake Tahoe. Until this extraordinary picture was taken, residents wondered why this overhead light kept going out.

Psychic manifestation in a graveyard is simulated by the creative camera of photographer Gordon Alexander.

Irene moved closer to talk softly with Mrs. Richard and Melody. I had been inside the small room with Irene, Mrs. Richard, Melody, and Joan Hurling. Glenn and Dick Mezzy had been just outside the door of the back room.

"Hey, Brad," Glenn whispered. "We've got something weird going on with this door."

I frowned an unspoken question, and Glenn went on to explain. "Well, you've been too busy recording and making notes on the conversation inside the room to notice, but the door keeps closing on you people."

"What do you mean?" I asked, looking with fresh vision on the wooden door.

"First of all," Mezzy said, "from the angle in which it is set, it should naturally swing open. See there? The floor slants a bit here, and the door jamb really isn't too cool a job. It would be an uphill fight against gravity for this door to close by itself."

"But," I said, supplying the cue line.

"But the door has been swinging closed," Glenn said. "A couple times, just as I've tried to take a picture of you in the back room, the door has swung nearly shut and ruined my shot. Another time, I wedged my toe under the door to hold it, and the darn thing nearly bent at the top because there was so much pressure being exerted against it!"

"Okay," I grinned. "We're all out of the room now. Shut the door if that is what it wants so badly."

Glenn swung the door to the jamb, then found he had to lift it to make a tight fit. "Now the blame thing should be happy," Glenn said, "it's stuck closed good and tight." The troublesome door firmly closed, we moved to join the others, who were walking toward the other end of the basement where the image of the baby's face had been set into the wall.

"Don't touch it!" Melody was shouting, as I joined Irene next to the strange effigy. "Don't touch it! It's evil. If you touch it, he'll come out of the wall. He'll come to kill again!"

Once again the resourceful Dick Mezzy was there to grasp the teenager's arm and pacify her. Melody's breathing had become very rapid. Her eyes were half-closed. She appeared about to enter a trance state.

"Listen to Mrs. Hughes!" Mezzy said sharply. "Listen to her! That baby's face can't hurt you!"

"Don't allow yourself to become hysterical," Irene said in her soft voice. "You'll only give strength to whatever negative forces might possibly be harbored somewhere in this house.

"Now, this face," she said, directing her attention to the strange impression in the wall. "First of all, I get the impression that no one in this family did this, did they?"

"No," Mrs. Richard said, "it was here when we moved in."

Irene paused, then continued: "There is no baby buried under here or anything like that, but I have the feeling that it was done to commemorate a family's first child. The parents were so proud that they did this as kind of a monument to their first baby.

"Nothing will happen to you if you touch this face," she said, directing her comments to the distraught Melody. "See?" she asked, as her fingers lightly stroked the baby's round cheeks. "This was a work of love. I think it is extremely interesting that people would do something like this.

"It's not a real baby's face," the psychic continued. "And that's not a real baby's skull under it, even though it looks so real. I would say that it was probably carved in the 1930s. Do you know how old the house is, Mrs. Richard?"

"Through research," our hostess answered, "we have found that the house is about eighty-five years old, maybe, even older. There is a bit of confusion, but it seems the first record of this house goes back to 1880."

"I would say that it is older than that," Mrs. Hughes suggested.

"It could be," Mrs. Richard readily conceded. "The civic records back that far are a bit jumbled, and they may have got this place and the one down the street mixed up."

"Did you learn that the people who lived here and the people who lived down the street were relatives?" Mrs. Hughes asked.

"That's right" Mrs. Richard said. "They were."

"I feel" Mrs. Hughes went on, "that across from here and not very far away that the original owner of this house had some dealings in grain. I see large grain bins or elevators and it looks like flour or meal or something is coming from there."

"There were some old grain mills and bins not too far from here," Dick Mezzy offered offered, "but I don't know how we could trace the connection today unless we could find just the right old-timer."

At this point, it was decided to return to the first floor of the home. "How's the door?" I asked Glenn just before we started up the stairs.

"Shut as tight as a clam," he assured me.

Melody's bedroom was at the top and to the right of the basement stairs. Irene Hughes stopped suddenly in the middle of the teenager's bedroom, stringing our party in a line from Glenn and Dick Mezzy, still at the top of the basement stairs, to Joan Hurling, just entering the kitchen, the first room off Melody's bedroom.

The psychic paused, as if carefully sorting out the impressions that had begun to bubble up from her unconscious.

"Do you often feel that someone is peeking in that window at you?" she asked Melody.

"All the time!" Melody shuddered. "It's such an icky feeling!"

"What does he look like?" Irene wanted to know.

"I can never tell for sure," Melody said, her upper teeth worrying an edge of her lip.

Irene moved to a dresser. "There's a strange, almost electrical vibration near this piece of furniture."

"I have that same kind of feeling in that same spot," Mrs. Richard sighed. "And I've had several friends feel the same thing there."

"It feels like there is something moving underneath me!" Irene said loudly.

"I've felt it now for six years!" Mrs. Richard agreed, her handkerchief patting desperately at heavy beads of sweat.

Irene would soon share her feelings with us, and we would all be able to participate in an audible representation the "thing" moving beneath floor as well.

BAM! BAM! BAM!

It's right under me!" Mrs. Hughes shouted. "It's like somebody pushing, banging up the floor. Does everyone feel it...hear it?"

One would have to have lost feeling below his knees and have gone suddenly deaf not to have felt and heard the powerful series of knocks.

"Do you want to look in the basement?" Irene asked, but Glenn and Dick Mezzy were already pounding down the stairs.

I knew where they were heading, and I walked back to the head of the stairs and shouted down: "Well?"

"The door to the back room is wide open," Glenn called up.

"We couldn't tame that door or whatever is in the room that easily," Dick added. When the two men rejoined us, Dick said that he had felt a "force" push past him just seconds before the knocking had begun on the floor.

After the journalist had vocalized this admission, others who had been standing in line with the basement stairway said that they, too, had felt "something" rush by them.

"I'm getting another image of our man in the basement," Irene said. "He was seen in a mirror once, and the mirror was broken, because I see a new one being put in this room."

"That happened to me,"Melody spoke up without hesitation, in spite of the tremor in her voice. "I saw the guy standing behind me when I was combing my hair and looking in the mirror. And he was so ugly that I just smashed the mirror. When my dad replaced the mirror, I had him put it where it wouldn't reflect that basement door."

"He's a tall man," Irene went on. "And in spite of his rather unkempt appearance, he is really not so ugly."

Mrs. Richard had been silent for several minutes, but Irene's continued description of the spectral interloper from the basement caused her to re-enter the conversation.

"We see his shadow," she said quietly. "That shadow was the first thing that we had ever seen out of the ordinary in this house. I saw this man's shadow, his outline in this doorway...."

"He was standing up straight," Melody interrupted her mother. "He wasn't leaning over."

"The first time," Mrs. Richard said, regaining the floor, "I thought it was my husband coming home from work. I kept calling his name, and he didn't answer me, and I thought he was doing something just to frighten me. I kept calling and calling his name, but he wouldn't answer. Then I thought someone had broken in."

"It was terrible," Melody added. "Every time we see that shadow is terrible. I know that it is that big ugly man trying to get us, trying to pull us with him into the grave!"

I could see that Irene was visibly upset by the girl's extreme emotionality. She reached out as if to touch Melody, but the teenager shrank back.

"Melody," Irene said, "I feel I have to give a message especially for you. You are a very distrustful girl. I feel that no matter how many girlfriends you may have, you don't trust any of them, and you push them away from you. It seems as though you want to push everyone away from you.

The attractive girl lowered her large, fawn-like eyes, touched by the psychic's advice, yet apparently determined to resist absorbing any of her wisdom. Irene continued her attempt to penetrate the psychic wall that the girl had erected around herself.

"I feel that you are going to have to make some very important decisions about relationships very soon and that you really have to be very careful in these decisions and not become antagonistic. You are about to ruin a very beautiful friendship, and I feel that you have already had a parting with a very good friend."

"Jane Hanson," Melody supplied the name, the very utterance constituting her admission of guilt.

"Take a second look at yourself, would you please?" Irene told her. "You need to be cautious for your own personal happiness. I feel if you don't, you will regret your actions very much within a year."

"You certainly have her right!" Mrs. Richard said, the eerie haunting momentarily forgotten in her concern for her daughter's future.

"But it was Jane's fault," Melody whined, abnegating all responsibility. "It was all Jane's fault that we had that fight."

A bit sternly, Irene added the following postscript to her advice: "Within a year, you will need a doctor's care. You will regret it very much if you follow that young man to California. He doesn't intend to keep his promises to you. In October, you will have to make the final decision. Although I urge you to resist his offers, I fear that you will listen only to your emotions."

(According to a follow-up report, Melody left home in October to live with a young man who had promised to take the teenager to California to live with the hippies. When last heard of, the girl had been left pregnant and addicted to heavy drugs by her unfaithful lover.)

Irene walked over to the kitchen sink. "There is another man who comes to you sometimes when you are doing dishes. Is that true, Mrs. Richard?"

"Yes, yes," the woman admitted. "It's a frightening presence to me. Whenever I feel him next to me, I run out the door. I can't stay anywhere in this house for too long a time when I am alone."

"I don't think you should be frightened of this spirit," Irene told her. "I think that this man belongs to you. He is someone who has passed over and wants to come through to you. Because you do not understand these things, you have only fear when you sense his presence."

"I'm not sure what the presence is," Mrs. Richard said, shaking her head vigorously, "but I know that it is frightening!"

"This is not the man in the basement," Irene emphasized.

"This feels like a very different person. This feels more like your father."

"My father has been dead since 1959," Mrs. Richard told the psychic. "There have been times when I have felt his presence just before a crisis in the family."

"Before we entered this house tonight, Mrs. Richard," Irene said, "I said that someone had died of cancer in this house, and I felt sick for a few moments after we came in your door."

"My mother died of cancer in 1967," she answered. "She was here in May and died in July."

"When I feel her dying of cancer," Mrs. Hughes commented, "I see a large pecan tree."

"If it truly is my mother you feel," Mrs. Richard said, "she loved pecans!"

By now we had been in and out of every room in the house with the exception of the small utility room opposite the door through which we had entered the Richard home.

"I feel a fast heartbeat!" Irene said the moment she stepped into the room. "This was the room of the man who was stabbed in the basement."

"It was in this room that we see the moving light some nights," Mrs. Richard said. "We have never been able to explain it as being caused by any kind of reflection or any light source that we can account for. It moves across the room from that picture on the wall to the window, to that light fixture over there."

"This was once a bedroom," Irene said. "He used to sit and read beneath that picture for a while, then he would become restless and walk over to the window and stand looking out. After more lonely hours in his room, he would shut off the light and go to bed."

"This was a bedroom when we moved in," Mrs. Richard said.

"I really feel that this man was a construction worker or some kind of trained laborer," Irene said. "And I feel that he was stabbed either in this house or somewhere else and robbed for his money. It may have been that he was brought to the basement and to that back room while someone went to notify the authorities.

"But now I feel that his spirit considers this house his home, and that is why he keeps returning here," the psychic continued. "That is why you have seen his image coming out of the wall. That is why you have seen his shadow in the doorway as if he were coming home from work. And the blood pouring from the faucets is a reminder of the terrible way in which he was murdered. But please understand, he means no one any harm."

After Irene had offered a prayer and a meditation for the restless entity's peace of spirit, we left the house to enter a garage in the Richard's back yard. It was here, according to most reports, that a maddened husband had put a violent end to his wife with the blast from a shotgun. Since the medium had already picked up most of the impressions relating to the murder while she was in the house, she again asked for peace for the entities.

It would be ridiculous for us to say that we had "cured" a haunting or that we had effectively put a restless spirit or two to rest. It seemed apparent to us that the house did serve as a receptacle for paranormal phenomena. There was the door that would not stay either open or closed; there was the ghost of the unkempt man that had appeared in the back room of the basement and in the girl's bedroom; there was the blood that had flowed from the faucet in the basement; there was the thumping, thudding evidence of some kind of preternatural force in the teenager's bedroom.

The Richard house, in our opinion, was a kind of "psychic supermarket" with an extraordinarily wide range of phenomena co-existing within its walls. But we make no claim that Irene Hughes is some kind of mystical wizard capable of instant exorcism. The medium did leave the Richards with brief instructions as to how they might employ psychic self-defense against any unwanted spectral visitors, and she gave the mother and daughter private consultations designed to fortify them against the fear and hysteria that had begun to warp their perspective toward life in the old house.

"How do you feel about Mrs. Hughes and her ability to tune in on the manifestations in your home?" I asked Mrs. Richard just before we left their home. We had been keeping one eye on the clock so that we could be out of the house before her unknowing and unsympathetic husband returned from work.

"The impressions she picked up of the things that happen in this house were just exactly correct," she admitted. "The man in the basement, the shadows, the ghost that shook me awake, the blood in the faucet—all those things were correct.

"Now, of course," she added, "I don't know about all those names she mentioned. This is an old house and some of those families might have lived here long before us. But she came very close to all the names that I know used to live here."

As we left the Richard house with its gamut of psychical phenomena, Glenn turned to shake his head at the platinum-haired, smiling lady in the backseat of the station wagon.

"Irene," he said, "I don't know how you do it. It was really remarkable the way you managed to tune in on all those things in that house. But there was one thing you couldn't do."

"Oh," Irene frowned, seeming to do a mental inventory of the house before she went on: "What was that, Glenn?"

"Even you couldn't make that pesky door in the basement behave!"

I would probably have to yield somewhat to the spiritistic hypothesis in this home, but there were certainly strong elements of poltergeistic- psychokinetic haunting involved in this Nebraska manse. The disturbed teenager, so often a vital ingredient of poltergeist manifestations, was present, but then so were the possibilities of virulent memory patterns having been impressed upon the environment by two murders. The mother and her daughter felt a definite interaction with at least two spirit entities, and Irene seemed to sense them and describe them exactly as the women had seen them.

the hammering fist of calvados castle

The household of Calvados Castle had been disturbed by the strange, midnight noises that had echoed throughout the dark corridors. That morning, the master of Calvados thought that he had the answer to the nocturnal knockings and thumpings.

"Someone is obviously trying to frighten us away from the castle so that they might purchase the surrounding land at a fraction of its value," he announced to his coachman and gardener. "They have no doubt found entrance to the castle by means of some long forgotten passage. They probably think it a simple matter to drive a man away from an old castle that he has just inherited."

He had no sooner finished theorizing when they heard howling and barking from the two formidable watch dogs which he had recently purchased. Rushing to a window, the master of Calvados saw the two dogs directing their angry attention toward one of the thickets in the garden. "Aha," he smiled. "Our noisy midnight visitors tarried too long and have found themselves cornered by the dogs."

He unlocked his weapons case and thrust a rifle into the hands of his coachman and the gardener. He selected a double-barreled shotgun for his own use. "Come," he said, "we'll soon have the miscreants at gunpoint."

After the men had posted themselves at the edge of the garden, the dogs were urged to attack. The two brutes rushed into the thicket with vicious growls.There was a moment of silence, and then the hoarse canine rumbles of fury turned to plaintive whines and whimpers of terror. The dogs ran out of the thicket with their tails between their legs, and the master could not call them back.

"Well," he chuckled nervously as he cocked both hammers of his shotgun, "whoever is in there can't be that terrible. Come," he urged his servants, "let's find out."

Cautiously, the three men entered the thicket, their firearms cocked and ready. They found nothing—not a footprint, not a shred of clothing on a branch, absolutely nothing. "But, what," the master asked of his men after they had searched in all directions, "could have frightened the dogs so?"

His question was never answered to his satisfaction, but that October midnight had seen the beginning of one of the most prolonged and terrifying of all accounts of poltergeist phenomena. The disturbances which took place in the Norman castle of Calvados from October 19, 1875 to January 30, 1876 were written up and published in the *Annnales des Sciences Psychiques* in 1893 by M.J. Morice.

Although the master of Calvados kept a diary which could later be used as a documentary of the phenomena, he insisted that his family name not be mentioned in connection with the "haunting." He is, therefore, referred to in the narrative only as M. de X. His immediate family consisted of Mme. de X, and their son. The remainder of the household consisted of Abbe Y., tutor to the son, Maurice; Emile, the coachman; Auguste, the gardener; Amelina, the housemaid; and Celina, the cook. As we shall see throughout this book, the poltergeist is no respecter of persons; the greatest devilment took place in the Abbe's room.

On the evening of October 13th, Abbe Y. came down to the drawing room and presented himself to M. and Mme. de X. "My armchair just moved," he insisted. "I distinctly saw it move out of the corner of my eye."

If the strange incident of the watchdogs had not been so fresh in his mind, M. de X may have accused his son's tutor of too much after-dinner sherry. He calmed the Abbe and returned with him to his room. He attached gummed paper to the foot of the cleric's armchair and fixed it to the floor. "Call me if anything further should occur," M. de X. told the Abbe.

At about ten that evening, the master of Calvados was awakened by the ringing of the Abbe's bell. He got out of bed, and hurried to the man's room.

"The whole room has been moving about," the tutor whispered from his bed. He had pulled the covers up to the bridge of his nose and peeked out at his employer as if he were a frightened child.

M. de X. saw that the armchair had indeed moved about a yard and that several candlesticks and statuettes had been upset.

"And there have been rappings on my wall," the Abbe complained in a voice that quavered on the brink of hysteria.

M. de X. heard a door open behind him and turned to see Amelina peeping out from her room across the hall. Her face was pale. "That's right, sir," she said. "I heard the rappings, too."

The next evening, the manifestations did not confine themselves to the Abbe's room. Loud blows were heard all over the castle. M. de X. armed his servants and conducted a search of the entire building. They could find nothing.

It would be a pattern that they would repeat again and again as the poltergeist began its seige in earnest. Night after night, its hammering fist would pound on doors and rap on walls. The inhabitants of Calvados castle would not know a night of unmolested slumber for more than three months.

The curate of the parish arrived to witness the phenomena and was not disappointed. Neither was Marcel de X., who had come to try to determine the origin of the manifestations. That night, the sound of a heavy ball was heard descending the stairs from the second floor to the first, jumping from step to step.

The parish priest was also invited to stay a night in the castle. He heard the heavy tread of a giant descending the stairs and proclaimed the activity to be supernatural. Marcel de X. agreed with the priest. He had quickly concluded that this ghost would be a most difficult one to "lay" and had decided to leave Calvados Castle to the noisy spirit. He wished M. de X. the best of luck and returned to his home.

On Halloween, the poltergeist seemed to outdo itself with a display of prowess that kept the household from going to bed until three o'clock in the morning.

The center of the activity had now become the green room, and the phenomena seemed always to either begin or end with loud rappings in this empty room. The poltergeist now seemed to walk with a tread that "had nothing human about it. It was like two legs deprived of their feet and walking on the stumps."

It was during a violent November rainstorm that the poltergeist acquired a voice. High above the howl of the wind and the rumble of the thunder, the beleaguered household heard a long shriek.

"It's a woman!" Amelina, the housemaid, said. "It's a woman outside in the storm calling for help."

Again the cry sounded and everybody looked curiously at one another. "It certainly sounds like a woman," Mme. de X. agreed. "Look out the window and see if someone is outside," she told Celina, the cook.

Celina had just reached the window when the next cry sounded from within the castle. The members of the household gathered together as if seeking strength from their unity. "The doors are all bolted," the Abbe said softly. "I saw to it myself."

Three sorrowful moans sounded as the thing ascended the staircase. The men of Calvados left the sitting room to carefully inspect the castle. They found nothing. There was no woman in the castle, and no sign that anything had entered the castle from the storm. They heard no more sounds until everyone was awakened at 11:45 the next night by terrible sobs and cries coming from the green room. They seemed to be the sounds of a woman in horrible suffering.

During the next few nights, the activity seemed to become intensified and the cries of the sorrowful woman in the green room had become "shrill, furious, despairing cries, the cries of demons or the damned."

Shortly after the "weeping woman" had arrived to add to the confusion at Calvados, a cousin of Mme. deX., an army officer, appeared to pay them a visit. He scoffed at the wild stories the members of the household told him, and against all their pleas, he insisted upon sleeping in the green room.

"I have my revolver always at my side," he told them."If anything disturbs my sleep, it'll get a bullet in its hide!"

The officer strode boldly to the green room, left a candle burning as a night light, and went straight to sleep. He was awakened a short time later by what seemed to be the soft rustling of a silken robe. He was instantly aware that the candle had been extinguished and that something was tugging at the covers on his bed.

"Who's there?" he demanded gruffly, lighting the candle at his bedside. The candle had no sooner flickered into flame when something extinguished it. Three times he lighted it, and three times he felt a cold breath of air blow it out. The rustling noise seemed to become louder, and something was defrnitely determined to rob him of his bedclothes.

"Declare yourself or I shall shoot!" he warned, cocking his revolver. The only answer to his demand was an exceptionally violent tug on the covers. He decided to shoot. It was a simple matter to determine where his silent adversary stood by the sound of the rustling and the pull on the bedclothes. The lead slugs, of course, struck nothing but the wall, and he dug them out with a knife that next morning. For some reason, however, the poltergeist did leave his covers alone for the rest of the night.

The Abbe continued to fare the worst of any member of the household throughout the duration of the phenomena. No other room in the castle had to entertain such mobile furniture. Whenever the cleric left his room, he always made certain that the windows were bolted and his door was locked. The key to his room was secured to a leather thong which he kept belted to his waist. These precautions never accomplished the slightest bit of good.

Upon returning to his room, the Abbe would inevitably find his couch overturned, the cushions scattered about, his windows opened, and his armchair placed on his desk. Once he tried nailing his windows closed. He returned to find the windows wide open, and by way of punishment, the couch cushions were balanced precariously on the outside window sill. Such pranks the Abbe could bear with much more patience than the time the poltergeist dumped every one of his books on the floor. Only the Holy Scriptures remained on the shelves.

The most vicious attack on the clergyman occurred once when he knelt at his fireplace stirring the coals, preparatory to placing new kindling on the andirons. Without warning, a huge deluge of water rushed down the chimney, extinguishing the fire, blinding the Abbe with flying sparks, and covering him with ashes.

The tutor woefully concluded that such actions could only be the work of his satanic majesty, the Devil.

The only other person who actually suffered physical pain dealt out by the poltergeist was Mme. de X. She was in the act of unlocking a door when the key suddenly disengaged itself from her grip and struck her across the back of her left hand with such force that she bore a large bruise for several days.

One night the invisible creature roamed the corridors as if it were a lonely wayfarer seeking admittance to the rooms of each of the members of the household. It knocked once or twice on the doors of several bedrooms, then, true to pattern, it paused to deal forty consecutive blows to the Abbe's door before it returned to thump about in the green room.

A priest from a neighboring parish heard the distinctive sounds of an animal rubbing itself along the walls when he ventured to stay the night in Calvados Castle. Another visitor once witnessed an evening of especially prolonged walking on the part of the poltergeist. "The steps were quite unlike human steps," he later wrote. "No animal could walk like that; it was more like a stick jumping on one of its ends."

The weary household had its only respite during the long seige when the Reverend Father H. L., a Protestant Canon, was sent there by the Bishop. From the moment the Reverend Father entered the castle until the moment he left, there was not the slightest sound from the noisy nuisance. But after the clergyman had made his departure, "...there was a noise as of a body falling in the first-floor passage, followed by that of a rolling ball giving a violent blow on the door of the green room..." and the poltergeist had once again begun his devilment in earnest.

On January 20, 1876, M. de X. left for a two-day visit to his brother, leaving his wife to keep up the journal. Mme. de X. records an eerie bellowing, like that of a bull, which bothered everyone during the master's absence. A weird drumming sound was also introduced during M. de X.'s absence, and a sound "something like strokes with a wand on the stairs."

Upon the master's return to Calvados, the poltergeist became more violent than it had ever been before. It stormed into the rooms of Auguste and Emile and turned their beds over. It whirled into the master's study and heaped books, maps, and papers on the floor. The midnight screams increased in shrillness and urgency and were joined by the roaring of a bull and the furious cries of animals. A rhythmic tapping paraded up and down the corridors as if a small drum and bugle corps were conducting manuevers. The rappings seemed to direct themselves, for the first time, to the door of Maurice, the son of M. and Mme. de X. Terrible screams sounded outside his room, and the vioience of the successive blows on his door shook every window on the floor.

On the night of Jnnuary 26th, the parish priest arrived with the intention of conducting the rites of exorcism. He had also arranged for a Novena of Masses to be said at Lourdes which would coincide with his performance of the ancient ritual of "putting a spirit to rest."

The priest's arrival was greeted by a long, drawn-out cry and what sounded like a stampede of hoofed creatures running from the first floor passage. There came a noise similar to that of heavy boxes being moved, and the door to Maurice's room began to shake as if something demanded entrance. The last days of the poltergeist are significant in that a great deal of the activity began to center around the adolescent son. It was as though the psychic tremors of puberty had somehow set the manifestations in motion or had reactivated unseen forces that had lain dormant in the old castle.

The rites of exorcism reached their climax at 11:15 on the night of January 29th. From the stairway came a piercing cry, like that of a beast that had been dealt its death blow. A flurry of rappings began to rain on the door of the green room. At 12:55, the startled inhabitants of Calvados Castle heard the voice of a man in the first-floor passage. "It seemed to cry twice Ha! Ha!" M.de X. records in his journal. "Immediately there were ten resounding blows, shaking everything all around. One blow on the door of the green room. Then the sound of coughing in the first-floor passage."

The "sound of coughing" may very well have been the poltergeist's death-rattle. The family rose and cautiously began to move about the castle. The priest slumped in exhaustion, sweat beading his forehead from the long ordeal. There was no sound of the hammering fist, no raucous screams, no shaking of doors, no shifting of furniture. They found a large earthen-ware plate which had been broken into ten pieces at the door to Mme. de X.'s room. No one had ever seen the plate before that night.

"Everything has stopped," M. de X. wrote in his journal.

His elation was somewhat premature. Several days after the exorcisms had been performed, Mme. de X. was sitting at a writing desk when an immense packet of holy medals and crosses dropped in front of her on her paper. It was as if the poltergeist had suffered a momentary setback and was announcing that it must retreat for a time to recuperate and lick its wounds.

Toward the end of August, soft knockings and rappings began to be heard. On the third Sunday in September, the drawing-room furniture was arranged in horseshoe fashion with the couch in the middle.

"The Devil has held council and is about to begin again," a parish priest was heard to moan.

A few days afterward, Mme. de X. lay terrified in her bed and watched the latch to her room unbolt itself. M. de X. was out of the castle for a few days on business, and she was alone with the servants.

The duration of the phenomena was much briefer this time, and the poltergeist seemed to be content to play the organ and to move an occasional bit of furniture about the room of Maurice's new tutor. Eventually the phenomena became weaker and weaker until the only thing that haunted Calvados castle was the memory of those terrible months when a poltergeist ran rampant in its corridors.

dark shadows in the magic theater of ufos

D r. Henry Lazarus'* involvement with the paranormal began when he became interested in UFOs.

Although he had pooh-poohed "flying saucers" in a kind of orthodox reflex action, he had occasion one weekend in October of 1971 to be staying at a hotel in Chicago where a UFO conference was being held. He had been amused by some of the convention-eers in the lobby—men with antennae fixed to their heads, spacey-eyed women dressed in flowing gowns—but then he chanced to glance at the program roster.

In addition to questionable presentations on visits to Venus and conversations with flying saucer pilots, he was surprised to see the names of a number of rather prominent astronomers, physicists, psychiatrists, and authors who were scheduled to give lectures on what seemed to be *bona fide* subjects relative to speculations on extraterrestrial visitations to Earth.

---

*In this chapter I have changed names, altered places, and dramatized certain aspects of the cases for what will soon be revealed as obvious reasons.

He had a few hours to kill, so he decided to buy some tickets and listen to a couple of the more lucid sounding speeches. He could, after all, leave in three minutes if his scientific sensibilities should be offended.

Not only did he become intrigued, rather than insulted, he found that he had become hooked by the whole area of UFO research.

His credentials easily bought him access to an all-night bull session with those members of the scientific community who dared association with the lunatic fringe in order to pursue an area of inquiry which they were convinced was of paramount importance to the planet's continued existence. Lazarus found that he was totally enthralled by these men and women who had immersed themselves in a field of research that challenged the scientific paradigm of the twentieth century.

Henry Lazarus' next step had been to fly to Boston to proselytize UFOs to his old friend Benjamin Chiang, an esteemed university professor of physics. Chiang had always been one of the most open-minded individuals whom Lazarus had ever encountered, and his response to Lazarus' presentation of the subject had been customarily direct. Instead of relying upon secondary reports, why did they not travel to a scene of alleged UFO activity and collect their own primary data?

Lazarus was pleased with his friend's reasonable suggestion, and he was excited by the proximity of such an area of alleged phenomena. One of the researchers at the Chicago conference had told him of a small town not far from Springfield, Massachusetts, where it was claimed that UFO manifestations could be observed almost nightly. The town was situated on the Connecticut River in the Holyoke Mountain Ridge, and it was only a few hours' drive from Boston.

Chiang had only a morning class on Wednesday, the next day. Why procrastinate? They could be on the road before noon and arrive on the scene in plenty of time to witness whatever activity the UFO-nauts had in store for them. Since his first class on Thursday was not until after lunch, they could afford the time to stay overnight if the phenomena put in a late appearance.

Chiang asked if Henry would mind if they asked a friend of his, a very skeptical, hard-nosed professor of biology, to accompany them if his schedule were compatible with such an expedition. In true scientific spirit, Lazarus welcomed a closed mind as a kind of control.

Two hours outside of Boston on the following day, Henry had begun to regret extending his permission to invite Dr. Philip Reisman along on the excursion. Reisman was more than a skeptic, he was a cynic. But it was fall, a beautiful October day, and the dazzling display of leaves in the brilliant autumn colors enabled Lazarus to tune out the dreary arrogance of the biologist.

By three that afternoon, with only a couple of comfort stops, they had found their UFO harbor. As was to be expected, it looked just like any number of small New England river towns in the sun of an autumn day.

Henry remembered that his informant had said that there was a woman at the local newspaper who had become an authority on the UFO and the creature sightings that had been made in the area over the past twenty years. He could not remember her name, but they ventured that she would not be hard to identify to what appeared to be a four-or-five-staff-member newspaper.

When Henry and Ben inquired at the newspaper office for the local UFO expert, the jolly, round-faced woman in her fifties who stood facing them readily admitted that she was the one who fit that description. Her name was Mary Higgins, and being a widow with a very limited social life, she unhesitatingly accepted their invitation to dinner in exchange for her guiding them to one of the more favored UFO-spotting sites.

Mrs. Higgins seemed only mildly impressed by their academic and professional credentials. She had, within the prior four months, brought two astronomers, five magazine writers, an Air Force officer, a documentary filmmaker, and an author of books on the paranormal to the same site to which she would guide them that evening.

Mary Higgins proved to be a delightful raconteur over dinner at the charming riverfront restaurant. She told them that the phenomenon often left scorched circles in the farmers' fields. Some farmers claimed that the UFOs appeared with such regularity over their meadows that they could set their watches by them.

At least half a dozen men and women claimed to have been taken on board the craft, and they all described the UFOnauts as being no more than five feet tall with large heads, big eyes with catlike pupils, hardly any noses to speak of, just a couple of slits for mouths, and pointed ears.

No, she answered Phil Reisman's jibe, they were not green-skinned, but they had been wearing green-colored, one-piece jumpsuits.

Each time Reisman spoke, Mrs. Higgins looked at him with the thinly veiled disgust one reserves for someone who repeatedly breaks wind at a dinner party.

All in all, the little New England river town and its surrounding environs seemed like a perfectly mixed cauldron of continually bubbling paranormal phenomena. For at least the last twenty years—and before that if the old-timers could be believed—there had been regular manifestations of UFOs, UFOnauts, Big Foot, Cat People, Giant Birdmen, ghosts, phantoms, and poltergeists. Grimly, she said in addition to the bizarre parade of creatures and celestial visitors, there had been a number of strange, unexplained disturbances.

Mrs. Higgins favored the theory that she lived in what some physical researchers termed a "window area," an aperture between dimensions of reality, so to speak. A place where, in what seemed to be cyclical patterns, mysterious phenomena continued to appear, then disappear. More aware intelligences, such as the UFOnauts, made use of such window areas to enter and to leave our Space-Time continuum.

Philip Reisman stated his opinion that it all sounded dangerously akin to madness to his way of thinking, and at that moment, in what may have been the purest of coincidences or a remarkable demonstration of mind over matter on the part of Mrs. Higgins, the waiter lost his footing and spilled an entire pitcher of ice water over Reisman's head. Whatever the cause of his dousing, the event was to serve as an omen of Reisman's baptism into a world he had denied could ever exist.

That night at the very stroke of twelve, as beautifully choreographed as if George Pal, Ray Harryhausen, Willis O'Brien, Douglas Trumbull, or any other of the great Hollywood special-effects masters were producing live-action theater, a glowing UFO appeared above the clump of trees before which Chiang parked his Volvo.

Lazarus felt fully alive for the first time in his life. Chiang was chortling with excitement. Mary Higgins was staring smugly at Philip Reisman, who was saying absolutely nothing, who seemed totally transfixed by the tableau before him.

The Volvo could not contain them. Lazarus flung open the door as if he were his Biblical namesake throwing back the stone before his tomb. Chiang was already racing across the open meadow that lay before the grove in which the UFO appeared to have settled.

"Don't rush it, boys," Mary Higgins warned them. "Don't get too close. Give it a minute."

Reisman shouted at them to come back, to be careful.

When they were about halfway across the meadow, two balls of greenish light moved out from the grove and came toward Chiang and Lazarus. The two physicists slowed their pace and looked curiously at the lights hovering above them.

Mrs. Higgins had stepped out of the car, and she was yelling to them that they were being monitored. Chiang and Lazarus felt that she might be correct.

And as they stood there, not wanting to offend or to transgress any rules they could not hope to comprehend, they heard the crushing footsteps of unseen entities moving in the grove ahead of them. To their right, they heard what seemed to be heavy breathing. To their left, the mumble of hollow, alien voices.

Chiang lifted his arms and shouted into the darkness that he was a man of goodwill and peace. Motivated by his friend's example, Lazarus did the same.

At that moment, the harsh, blaring, horribly discordant sound of the car horn shattered the almost reverential attitude of the two scientists toward the promise that lay beyond them in the grove of trees. The sound of the horn became the shriek of a frightened, demented beast, and it seemed to echo around them in a hundred variations of disharmony.

From the very first note of the metallic scream, every aspect of the UFO manifestation seemed to shrink back, as if the footsteps, the lights, the breathing, the voices were but multiple probings of a single entity—an entity that had now begun to retreat, to withdraw, like a wild thing startled by the blare of a hunter's trumpet.

In the matter of a very few seconds, all facets of the phenomena had seemingly been pulled back to the grove, and Chiang and Lazarus stood in the center of the meadow in anguish, as the UFO shot up into the night sky at a rate of speed that they could not comprehend in terms of the science which they understood. They felt alone, disappointed, like two small children who had only caught a glimpse of Santa's boot , the gift-laden elf disappeared up the chimney.

When they returned to the Volvo, they demanded to know why Dr. Reisman had pressed on the horn. His reply was barely distinguishable through his frightened, chattering teeth, but it had something to do with saving them from being taken into a spaceship and chopped up for food.

Mrs. Higgins' face in the light from the headlamps bore an expression composed of nearly equal parts of contempt and pity for the biologist.

"It's scared away now," she told Chiang and Lazarus. "You might just as well call it a night."

They drove Mary Higgins back into town and thanked her for her graciousness and her tolerance.

When they went in search of a motel that might still be open, Philip Reisman insisted that they return at once to Boston. Lazarus and Chiang acquiesced, since another day spent with the man would have been intolerable to both of them.

They were not five miles out of town when Reisman, who was sitting in the backseat, began to shout that they were being followed by two glowing green lights.

When Chiang glanced in the rearview mirror, he was excited to see that Reisman was correct.

Lazarus clutched his friend's shoulder and together, almost as one, they uttered a shared wish that they might have another opportunity for interaction with the UFO occupants.

But then the lights whooshed by them, one on either side, and vanished into the darkness.

By the time Chiang and Lazarus dropped Reisman his apartment, the man was nearly hysterical. He had cowered in a corner of the backseat most of the way home, his teeth chattering, his eyes weeping. He had shouted out a dozen times at imagined monsters at the side of the highway.

When they walked into Chiang's apartment thirty minutes later, the telephone was ringing.

It was Reisman, babbling into the receiver about something pounding on his walls.

Ben was about to tell him to take some tranquilizers and to go to sleep when a remarkable thing occurred. A mysterious pounding began on the walls of his own apartment.

At this point, Reisman screamed that a dark, hooded figure had appeared in the corner of his bedroom.

Almost as soon as Chiang repeated for Lazarus' benefit what the man had said, the two of them were gasping at the materialization of a dark, hooded figure in a corner of Ben's living room.

Before either of them could assimilate that phenomenon, the radio unit in the stereo console clicked on, and some unseen agency moved the dial from station to station. Three books were made airborne from the shelf where they had rested. The refrigerator door popped open. All the water faucets in the kitchen and the bathroom were turned to full steam.

The weird, pointless manifestations disrupted both apartments until dawn, about two hours after they had begun.

"We had undergone quite an initiation that night," Henry Lazarus told me later. "And the phenomena continued, even at long distance. I would be in Houston talking to Ben back east in Boston, and he would say, 'Hey, there's that dark hooded figure standing in the corner again,' and, son of a gun, if I wouldn't see a similar figure standing inside my closet door or over in a corner of my bedroom."

Chiang pushed his chair back from the table around which we had been drinking coffee late into the night. "Well, what we theorize occurred is that we somehow activated a reflexive response from a concentration of UFO energy, the X-Force, in that community."

"I would say," Lazarus speculated, "that the negative factor was Reisman's fear and resultant hysteria. His emotional reaction to the phenomenon overrode our scientific curiosity."

Henry Lazarus continued the speculation: "We feel that there had been a genuine UFO landing near that village at some undetermined time in the past. It was quite likely witnessed by one or more townspeople. This incident became so important to the psyches of the men and women in that rather remote area that their collective energy began to create a phantom by the conduit of their group mind.

"The more energy they invested in the archetype of the UFO experience, the more solid and material it became.

"The more material it became, the more people who witnessed it coming into being, the stronger the phantom of the real UFO experience became."

What had happened to Dr. Reisman, the cynical biologist who had his perimeters of reality so broadly stretched for him?

"I regret to say," Chiang sighed deeply, "that Philip Reisman's life became a tragic comedy. A rigidly closed mind did not serve him well. It is best to be at least somewhat open to all aspects of existence, so that when you come face of face with something that has not previously been a part of your reality, you can deal with it without shattering into mental and emotional fragments.

"Dr. Reisman had to resign his post with the university. He became a 'born again' Christian and walked the streets of Boston distributing fundamental Christian literature. The last we heard of him, he was living in a commune in Maine, attempting to chant the nature spirits into helping him grow giant vegetables."

Bill Fogarty began by telling me that he had seen a UFO in April of 1972, when he had been twenty years old. He had been a college junior at the University of Indiana at South Bend, a member of an informal group that got together once a week to discuss politics, philosophy, art, poetry, and women.

One night someone had brought up the topic of UFOs—and that very evening, driving back to their respective apartments, five of their number claimed to have witnessed a low UFO overflight.

Fogarty assured me that each of the five—and he had been one of them—were all college students, physically fit, non-drinkers, no drug users, and two of them were Vietnam combat veterans. Each of them prided himself on maintaining a cool, analytical approach to all aspects of life, especially toward anything that smacked of the occult or the bizarre. And yet each of them swore that he had seen what was unmistakably an object in the sky that he could not identify as a conventional aircraft, an ordinary celestial manifestation, a weather balloon, a bird, or anything that could have been flying above them.

Four nights later, two of the five had seen another UFO. Then, on the next evening, Fogarty and the other two saw a brightly glowing object overhead as they returned around one o'clock from a movie.

The five decided to form a splinter group in order to discuss the UFO phenomenon. They were well aware that the main group of culture vultures would mock them for their flying saucer experiences and make light of the entire subject, so they would head for an all-night pancake house to compare notes and thoughts on their subjective response while undergoing the experience of encountering what appeared to be an unknown phenomenon.

Fogarty said that it had not been long before the five of them had a group sighting, and from that evening on they had taken to nightly skywatches.

"We all witnessed UFOs cavorting in the midnight sky," Fogarty said. "On one occasion I stood within ten feet of two nocturnal lights hovering silently in midair. Later, we heard rappings in the dark, hollow voices, heavy breathing, and the crushing footsteps of unseen entities.

"Strangely enough," Fogarty said, smiling, "we were able to maintain our cool toward all the phenomena occurring around us. Maybe we got to thinking that we had been chosen for some special kind of interaction. Perhaps, secretly, we were beginning to view ourselves as masters of two worlds. I mean, we were all Dean's List students, all athletic young men, normally balanced emotionally, mentally, sexually. I guess we felt that modern Renaissance men such as ourselves could deal rationally with such phenomena and stay in control of the situation."

But then, Fogarty went on, the manifestations had become violent. They had swept through one of the group's home one night, pounding on the walls, yanking furiously at the bedposts, striking the startled young man in the face, terrorizing his entire family. Some of the group were followed by unmarked automobiles that seemed a bizarre mixture of styles and models—phantom automobiles, if you will.

Within the next few months, the number of harrowing incidents had increased and had expanded to include strange, dark-clad, nocturnal visitors in the apartments of several of the group members.

Radio and television sets switched on by themselves. Doors opened and closed—although, when tested, they were found to have remained locked. One of the group made the wild claim that he had been teleported one night from his bedroom to the middle of a forest on the outskirts of the city.

"As preposterous as that sounds," Fogarty said, "I'm sure that most of us accepted it as true, since we had all undergone some incredible experiences. We had all lost our sense of perspective. I began sleeping with the light on and a .38 Special under my pillow. Another of my friends invested heavily in weapons and began running with a group that offered sacrifices to Odin. A third was 'born again' into fundamental Christianity. The other two dropped out of college a month before they would have graduated with honors."

What did he think it had all meant?

Fogarty considered the question carefully. "I've thought a lot about that. I think the five of us had entered a kind of game, a contest, a challenge, a testing experience. The trouble was, we just don't know all the rules.

"Modern society doesn't prepare us to play those kind of games. Modern society doesn't tell its kids that there is another reality around them. Our educators have ignored the individual mystical experience and the other dimensions that can open up to those who enter altered states of consciousness—whether it be through drugs or through accidentally stumbling into the twilight zones."

Is humankind involved in some kind of continuing interaction with the "Other"?

Is it the same ancient intelligence that continually tests us, or do new teams come to play the reality game with us?

"I had the feeling," Fogarty recalled, "that my friends and I were dealing with some kind of energy. At first I thought it was something from outer space, some alien world. But I've thought about our experiences a great deal over the past eleven years, and I believe that we had somehow activated some energy that is a part of this planet. I think we might have triggered some kind of archetypal pattern with our minds. Maybe that's what magicians have tried to do since Cro-Magnon days—interact with and control that energy with their minds."

How had such intelligent, resourceful young men lost control? Why had they ended up paranoid, frightened, or converted?

"Because we weren't magicians, obviously," Fogarty chuckled. "We had no idea just how deadly serious the game could become. It really is a game for wizards, not for smart-ass college students who believe their brilliant intellects and their physics books can provide an answer for everything."

Jim Hunter's father had been a senior sales representative for an import company based in the South Pacific. The company was always shifting the Hunters around, but from March of 1964 to May of 1968, they had lived in New Zealand.

Shortly after he had turned seventeen on March 12, 1967, Hunter had gone on holiday at the beach near the little New Zealand ocean town of Kawhai and had been swimming around a section of shoreline that was not usually penetrated by tourists. It was here that he found a flat, smooth metallic object under a tidal rock.

The object was oval-shaped, smooth, rounded at the edges, and engraved with peculiar symbols. It weighed about one pound, and when he found it, it had been tightly wedged between two tide-level boulders that were only exposed at low tide. The object looked very old. Algae and other sea deposits encrusted it.

When such objects are found in New Zealand, they are most often taken for Maori relics, which are in high demand. Hunter's father immediately advised him to take it to a knowledgeable Maori to have it examined.

Two weeks went by, during which time the object passed from hand to hand among Maoris who were experienced in appraising the relics of their people. At last the consensus was delivered to Hunter: The object did not come from anything or any time in their culture.

A man who represented himself as a journalist for the *New Zealand Herald* claimed that he had heard of the object from a Maori contact, and he asked if he might see it. After a few minutes' examination, he expressed his feelings that the object was made of some kind of bronze alloy, and he asked if he might take it to Auckland for some tests.

Hunter refused his request, for his father had already spoken to a friend at the university in Christchurch about the possibility of having a metallurgical analysis run on the object. Hunter could not recall if such an analysis had ever been made, but he did remember that the curio ended up in a dresser drawer in their home in Te Awamutu, where it was to remain until his father received orders to move to New York in May of 1968.

"That was when I first discovered that the object was missing," Hunter told me. "I knew very well the drawer in which it had rested for nearly a year, but when I came to pack it for moving, it was not there. It had disappeared."

Chagrined, slightly suspicious of one or two friends who might have envied his find, Hunter had nothing to do but to accept his loss.

As they waited for their flight from Auckland International Airport in May, Hunter was approached by two young Polynesian types, who claimed to be from New Zealand Inland Revenue. They asked him if he were taking anything illegal out of the country, and they were especially interested in learning if he had any relics, art objects, or the like.

Hunter's parents were saying good-bye to friends some distance from him, and since the men acted very professional, he had become intimidated by them. He did his best to explain that he had no relics in his possession, but then the two men insisted that he go with them to a hotel in Auckland to undergo a private baggage check. It was at that point that he had summoned his father.

Hunter's father demanded to see their identification and asked why they couldn't examine his son's baggage right there in the airport. When their answers didn't make sense, his father had summoned a patrolling constable to intervene. His mere arrival seemed to scare the two away, and they shuffled off without other word. The whole incident had seemed very shady and frightening to Hunter.

That fall, back in the United States, Hunter had enrolled in Columbia University for his freshman year. Shortly after the term had begun, he was approached in his room by a middle-aged Italian art dealer who said that he had heard that Hunter had spent some time in New Zealand and that he was interested in purchasing any relics or curios that Hunter might have brought with him.

Although the alleged art dealer was polite and businesslike, he was annoyingly persistent. In spite of Hunter's repeated denials that he had any such relics to sell him, the man had approached him three times before the winter holidays.

Through correspondence, Hunter had learned that three of his closest friends in New Zealand had been questioned by men who seemed to fit the description of the two who had attempted to search his luggage at the airport. In one instance, the New Zealand police had to be called in to block continued harassment. In another case, a girl's life had been threatened.

According to their letters to him, each of his friends had been questioned about whether or not Hunter had given them anything to keep before he had left New Zealand. They all used words like "spooky," "weird," and "creepy" to describe the men who had talked to them.

In 1970, Hunter had transferred to Stanford University. He had no sooner moved into his apartment and had the telephone installed when he received a call warning him never to return to New Zealand.

During a later call, a woman with a high-pitched voice had informed Hunter that he was being kept under surveillance by a group who felt that he had acted unjustly in the past by not returning things to their proper owners.

In 1972, Hunter had decided to teach high school for a time before he continued with his graduate work. That summer, a few weeks before he was to begin his first job in the Sacramento school system, he was vacationing in San Francisco. Late one night, the telephone rang, and it was a jovial, laughing man, who said that Hunter had acted wisely by not returning to New Zealand.

"You must understand what a quiet life I led as an undergraduate," Hunter said. "Yet at both Columbia and at Stanford I probably received thirty or more telephone calls from anonymous voices advising me not to return to New Zealand or reprimanding me for having taken something that did not belong to me. I didn't wear an armband declaring that I had lived in New Zealand for four years, and I seldom discussed my life there with any but a few of my closest acquaintances. Who could possibly have cared about my having found that metallic slab? And who could possibly have taken such a long-term interest in me because of a casual act committed a few days after my seventeenth birthday?"

About the third day after classes had begun in the suburban community of Sacramento where Hunter had accepted a high school teaching position, a student unknown to him had stopped by his room to say hello. Hunter knew that such an act was hardly unusual, since students will often do this to look over a new teacher. But from the first, the boy acted strangely inquisitive.

Hunter was astonished when the teenager stepped to the blackboard and drew the same design that he had first seen on the mysterious object that he had found in New Zealand. He smiled to Hunter, then asked him if he knew what the symbols meant.

When Hunter pressed him, in turn, for some answers, the boy erased the design, laughed, and said that he was just fooling around, that he did not mean anything by it.

"I never saw the kid again," Hunter said. "I described him to a couple of the other teachers and to a bunch of students, but no one was able to identify him. I doubt very much if he actually went to the school at all."

Did he still receive calls about the object?

"I hadn't been at the university more than four days when someone rang my room and scolded me about taking things that didn't belong to me," Hunter replied. "I came here in the fall of 1976 to begin my doctorate program. I had been awarded a teaching assistantship, and I felt very much together with life. Then that damn telephone call came."

What exactly did it say?

"It said that I should never take anything from where I had found it," Hunter recalled. "It said that I should always leave things where they were. That I had no right to act unjustly and to take things away from their proper owners!"

bizarre honeymoons

Should the reader be willing to accept that young people in the throes of marital adjustment are capable of setting certain paranormal phenomena into psychokinetic motion, then he can imagine the phenomena that might be produced by *three* newlywed couples living under the same roof. Author M. G. Murphy provided the editors of *Fate* with a notarized affidavit certifying to the authenticity of the eerie events described by the six participants of such a haunted honeymoon.

The Murphys (author Murphy's parents), the Nelsons and the Chapmans found themselves with a common problem in February of 1917: the scarcity of money. They decided to find a house large enough so that each couple would have their own bedroom, then cut down on expenses by sharing the rent. After a period of house-hunting, they found an immense three-story house on the outskirts of Santa Ana, California, which rented for an absurdly small sum.

It took little time for the three couples to settle, for none of them had much furniture, and, strangely enough, the mansion had been rented fully furnished. Mrs. Murphy was an avid student of antiques, and she was overwhelmed by the splendid treasures the house contained. It seemed incredible that one could even consider renting out such a magnificent house complete with such valuable antiques, but the three young couples were not about to argue with Providence.

A few days after they had moved in, the three young wives were interrupted in their polishing of the paneled doors by the sound of someone running up the stairs. They had the full length of the stairway in their sight, yet they could hear the unmistakable sounds of someone clomping noisily up the stairs. Their report of the incident that night at dinner brought tolerant smiles from their husbands.

Several nights later the household was jolted out of sleep by Mrs. Nelson screaming that something was trying to smother her. While her husband sat ashen-faced with fear, she wrestled with an invisible assailant, until, finally, she was thrown to the floor with such force that her ankle twisted sickeningly beneath her and her head hit the wall. The doctor who was called to treat Mrs. Nelson's injuries mumbled something about it not being surprising considering the house they were living in; then he would say no more.

Within the next few days the footsteps continued to sound up and down the stairway. The men heard them too, and they also heard slamming doors and the splashing of water faucets being turned on. One night everyone saw the huge sliding doors pushed open by an invisible hand, and they all felt a cold breeze blow past them. When they locked the doors that night, one of the men observed that they were really locking up to protect the outside world from what they had on the inside. He was rewarded for his flippant observation by an incredibly foul, nauseating odor which hung about the stairway for days.

The three couples held a council to decide whether or not they should move. Although the disturbances were somewhat annoying, they reasoned, the rent simply could not be bettered. They would bear the bizarre phenomena and save their money.

The morning after their council had voted in favor of frugality, a new manifestation occurred which may have been designed to make them reconsider their decision. At the first glimmer of dawn, the couples awakened to the sound of a heavy wagon creaking up the driveway. They could hear the unmistakable sounds of shod hooves, jingling harness, and the murmur of men's voices. The phenomena, which culminated in an argument between two ghostly men, occurred at least twice a week thereafter.

When the three couples still gave no sign of moving, yet another disturbance was added to the repertoire of the haunting. Again, just before dawn, clanking sounds could be heard coming from an old rusted windmill at the rear of the house. There came the sound of a falling body that struck the metal structure on its way down, then came to rest with a heavy thud on the ground.

Mr. Murphy learned from some townspeople that a hired man had once fallen to his death from atop the windmill when a sudden gust of wind had swung the fan loose from its stabilizing brake. Apparently the three couples were being treated to an audio replay of the tragedy on alternating mornings with the creaking wagon and the argument.

One of the husbands discovered yet another phenomenon when he went into the basement to get a jar of fruit. Something knocked him off a box as he stood on tiptoe, reaching for the highest shelf, then lay sighing in a dark corner of the fruit cellar. The other two men stopped laughing at their friend when they followed him back down into the basement and heard the thing sighing and panting like a giant bellows.

Mrs. Murphy's grandparents came for a visit, and Grandmother Woodruff was quick to notice that there were "people" in the room with them. Grandmother Woodruff was a tiny woman who possessed great psychic abilities. In spite of her husband's violent disapproval of such activity, she had gained a great reputation as a "rainmaker" and a levitator of furniture and household objects. Grandmother Woodruff pointed to the portrait of the blonde woman that hung above the fireplace and told the couples that the woman had been poisoned in one of the upstairs bedrooms. A frown from Grandfather Woodruff silenced her elaboration.

Later, when the others were gone, Mrs. Murphy asked her grandmother to attempt to gain additional psychic impressions. Grandmother Woodruff learned that something inhuman haunted the premises. "I'm not easily frightened," she said, "but whatever it is, I am terrified."

Just as the elderly couple were preparing to leave, some invisible monster threw Grandmother Woodruff to the floor before the fireplace and began to choke her. Grandmother's face was beginning to turn blue when Grandfather arrived to help her fight off the unseen foe. The thing slammed Grandmother to the floor when her husband called upon the name of God, and Grandfather Woodruff swept his gasping wife into his arms. Grandfather proclaimed the place a house of evil and advised them to move at once.

Grandmother Woodruff, whose voice was now but a rasping whisper, said that she had been "talking" to the blonde lady when she had seen an awful creature creep up behind her. "It was as big as a man, but like nothing I've ever seen before. It had orange hair standing out from its head, stiff and wiry. Its hands curved into talons. The arms were like a man's, but covered with orange hair." The beast had threatened to kill Grandmother Woodruff, and it had left cuts on her neck where its talons had gouged into her flesh. "I know that this house will burn down within a short time. Nothing will be left but the foundation," she warned her granddaughter.

The three couples decided to move a few days later after a night during which a huge black bat had crept under the bedclothes and clamped its teeth into Mrs. Nelson's foot. It had taken two men to beat and to pry the monstrous bat off her foot, and even after it had been clubbed to the floor, it managed to rise, circle the room, and smash a window to escape.

Within a few weeks after the newlyweds left the mansion, it burned to the ground. The Murphy family's involvement with the hideous entity had not ended, however.

Ten years after Grandmother Woodruff's death, several of her kin were living in her old ranchhouse in San Bernardino. Author Murphy's Uncle Jim came downstairs ashen-faced one night and said that he had seen an orange-haired "thing" poke its head out of the storage room, then shut the door. Although the family laughed at him, Uncle Jim later complained of "something" in his room at nights. The gales of derisive laughter ceased when Uncle Jim died.

In 1948, Murphy's parents, who had been one of the three couples who had honeymooned in the accursed mansion, decided to spend their vacation on Grandmother Woodruff's old ranch. For company, they had the author's nine-year-old son Mike with them. Everything seemed comfortable in the old homestead on that first night, until, about 3:00 A.M., Mrs. Murphy was awakened by something shufffing toward Mike.

According to Murphy: "Looking it full in the face, Mother saw a grinning mouth with huge, yellow teeth. Its eyes were almost hidden in a series of mottled lumps. Brushing her aside, it lunged toward Mike, who was now wide awake. Mother grabbed a handful of thick long hair and desperately clutched a hairy, scaly arm with the other. In the moonlight which shone through the window she saw huge hands which curved into long talons."

By this time Mike was sitting up in bed screaming, watching helplessly as his grandmother did battle with the grotesque creature. At last Grandfather Murphy turned on the light in his room and came running to investigate the disturbance. The monster backed away from the light, but continued to gesture toward Mike.

In the light Mrs. Murphy could see that the beast wore "...a light-colored, tight-fitting one-piece suit of a thin material which ended at knees and elbow." Bristly orange hair protruded from its flattened and grossly misshapen nose, and thick, bulbous lips drew back over snarling yellow teeth. It gestured again in Mike's direction, then turned and shuffled through the doorway, leaving behind a sickening odor of decay.

Whether the entity had been attracted to the young couples by the tensions of their marital adjustment or whether it had been somehow activated by the vibrations of the life force emanating from their sexual activity cannot be answered. Although the phenomena began with somewhat ordinary poltergeistic disturbances, they seem to have culminated in either the creation of, or the at- traction of, a violent and malignant entity. To the Murphys, at least, it has been demonstrated that creatures which haunt one house can, if they will it, move their operations along with the family. The old ranchhouse, the entity's last habitat, was razed in 1952.

Mrs. L. W. P. prepared a report of the manifestations which occurred in the small bungalow which she and her husband rented shortly after their marriage. They had only lived in the house about a week when she was disturbed by a strange thudding noise, "like someone striking an empty cardboard box with a closed fist." She heard the noise several times over the next two weeks, and once it sounded not more than a few feet above her head. She began to have fainting spells, and when she regained consciousness, she would feel weak and drained of strength. She resisted telling her husband about the bizarre disturbances for fear of inviting his mockery. Her husband was a very materialistic young man who would not listen sympathetically to tales of things that went "bump" in an empty house.

Then one night when the newlyweds were hosting another young couple, Mrs. L.W. P. heard her husband calling her and the other woman from the kitchen, where they had been preparing a snack. "There's someone in the house," he said excitedly. Their guest substantiated his claim, and the two young couples set about searching the small home.

Mr. P. had said that as he and the other man had been sitting in the living room discussing an incident which had happened at work that day, a tall, blonde, barefoot woman had pushed open the draperies and looked in at them. Her hair had seemed to be wet, and it stuck to her face. Both men had seen the woman clearly, and they had watched her bare feet under the draperies as she turned and walked away.

Since her husband had seen something for which he could not account, Mrs. L.W.P. unburdened herself and told them of the noises which had plagued her during the day and of the spells of fainting which had beset her in association with the thudding sounds.

"We lived in that house for just a few more weeks," Mrs. L.W.P. wrote in her account; "then we gave up and moved. We talked to a number of old-timers in the area who claimed that the place was haunted by the ghost of a woman who had been drowned by her husband. We were told that the place was always for rent or for sale. Many families had lived in the house, but none of them had stayed for more than a few weeks at a time."

Carol G. knew that, because of religious reasons, her grandfather did not approve of Jack S. courting her. Grandpa G. had strong convictions that one should marry within one's faith, and it may have been the psychological tension which her grandfather created within her unconscious that led to a flurry of poltergeist activity around the teen-age girl.

For a period of hearly two weeks Jack's visits to the house were accompanied by violent outbursts of psychokinetic energy. Mrs. G.'s favorite vase shattered as the two young people held hands on the sofa. Invisible hands banged on the piano keyboard, and the piano stool jumped across the living-room floor and struck Carol smartly across the shins. One night as the young lovers had just finished making a tray of cookies and were allowing them to cool, the entire two dozen smoldered into flame. As in most poltergeist attacks, the unconscious energy center of the disturbance received the brunt of its abuse and physical torment. Stigmatalike scratches were seen to appear on Carol's upper arms, and on one occasion, teeth marks appeared just below her shoulderblades.

"You're to blame for this," Grandpa G. said one night, advancing upon Jack with his cane. "To mix religions is to do the devil's work, and you've brought the devil upon us."

The old man swung his cane and caught Jack stoutly across the forehead. Jack jumped to his feet, dazed, angry, but restrained by his sweetheart. "If you were thirty years younger," Jack said, grimly clenching his fists.

The poltergeist activity eventually spent its psychic energy, and the vortex of paranormal disturbances subsided. In spite of Grandpa G.'s fulminations, Carol's parents were open-minded toward a religiously mixed marriage and gave their consent for the young people to be wed. Grandpa G. contracted pneumonia before the wedding date and passed away in an oxygen tent in the hospital. In spite of their differences over religion and her choice of a husband, Carol was genuinely sorrowful when the old man died.

A few psychic strands of unconscious guilt over marrying outside her religion and against her grandfather's wishes may have produced the phenomena that visited Carol on her wedding night.

The newlyweds had checked into the nearest possible motel, eager to consummate their marriage. They had no soon gone to bed, however, when they were sharply distracted from the marital rite by a loud knocking on the wall beside them. They tried desperately to ignore the sound, to blame it on a raucous party next door, but the more they listened to the rapping, the more they both realized that it sounded very much like Grandpa G.'s cane.

As they watched in amazement, a glowing orb of light appeared beside their bed. As the illumination grew and took shape, they were astonished to see a wispy outline of Carol's grandfather standing before them.

"He…he's smiling," Carol said, somehow managing to shape functional speech in her fear and surprise.

As the newlyweds lay in each other's arms, they saw the image of Grandpa G. smile, move his cane in the sign of the cross, then in a gesture of farewell. "He's blessed us, Jack," Carol said, tears welling in her eyes as she watched the ethereal form of her grandfather fade away. "He understands now that he's on the other side. Earthly differences don't matter over there."

Mrs. L.J.J. has prepared an account of an experience which occurred to her and her fiancé shortly before their marriage. They had gone to a movie, then decided to drive out to the tiny house in the country where they would live after they had celebrated their nuptials.

"It was fun to go there and plan our future," she said. "The house was on land that was too wooded to be good farmland, but we planned only to plant a small garden, and Karl would continue his job in town.

"We had only kerosene lamps in those days, but they always gave off such a cheery light—at least, they usually did. That night, when Karl lit the lamp, I had an eerie feeling that something was wrong, that we were not alone. Karl must have felt the same way as I did, because he kept looking over his shoulder, like he expected to catch sight of someone spying on us.

" 'I'm going to have a look around,' he said, trying to sound casual. He took the lamp, so I stayed right beside him. We walked through the small house, and Karl grinned at me sheepishly, as if he were apologizing for feeling uneasy in what was to be our honeymoon cottage.

"We heard a strange chattering, like some giant squirrel or chipmunk, coming from a dark corner in the room. It sounded unreal, unearthly, and a strange coldness passed over my body. 'Let's go, Karl,' I whispered. 'I'm frightened.'

"Before we could move toward the door, Karl suddenly threw his hands up over his head as if he were trying to grab something behind him. His head seemed pulled backward and to one side. His mouth froze in a grimace of pain and fear, and his eyes rolled wildly. He lost balance, fell to his knees, then to his side. He kicked over a chair as he rolled madly, fighting and clawing the air around his neck.

"I stood by helplessly, stunned with fear and bewilderment. Karl managed to struggle to his feet. His eyes bulged and he gasped fiercely for each breath. Some unseen thing seemed to be strangling him.

" 'The door...open...run to car...you drive,' he panted. We ran to the car, Karl stumbling, staggering as if something heavy and strong were perched atop his shoulders with a death grip about his throat. 'I...can't get...damned thing off!'

"I got behind the wheel of the car. 'Drive...fast!' Karl said, his hands desperately trying to pry the invisible monster's paws from his throat.

"I drove for about two miles down the road. Suddenly there was a blinding flash inside the car. A brilliant ball of fire about the size of a basketball shot ahead of our car, then veered sharply to the left and disappeared into a clump of trees.

"I did not stop all the way back to town. Karl lay gasping beside me, his head rolling limply on the back of the seat. He did not speak until we were back inside the city limits. 'It was some inhuman thing from the pits of hell,' he said. 'It was big, strong, and it would have killed me.' "

Mrs. L.J.J. concluded her account by writing that although they returned to their small home with some trepidation, they never again encountered that monstrous, invisible strangler that chattered like a giant rodent.

"you are mine to kill!"

When the sky began to grow black, Esther Cox asked Bob McNeal to take her home.

"Where's your adventurous spirit, girl?" McNeal laughed. "You wouldn't let a bit of rain spoil our buggy ride, would you?"

Esther leaned closer to her young man, as if she were trying to absorb some of his lightheartedness. She knew that he had gone to some expense to rent a horse and buggy so that he might take her riding outside of Amherst, but the darkening sky disturbed her.

"Don't worry," McNeal said, reading her concern. "The buggy has a hood that I can raise in case of a shower."

They had not gone far from the town when McNeal pulled into a small wood and set the brake on the buggy.

"Not tonight," Esther said, shrugging his arm from her shoulder. "Not when it looks like it is about to storm at any minute."

McNeal would not be put off and Esther allowed him to kiss her, then repeated her request that he take her home before it began to rain.

"We won't be going yet," McNeal told her. There was a strange set to his lips and his eyes seemed almost glazed. "We won't be going for quite a while."

Only nineteen, Esther was not very experienced in such situations, but she recognized McNeal's expression.

"Take me home at once, Robert McNeal," she said, trying to to sound firm and indignant although her voice quavered with fear.

"Not until you come into the woods with me," McNeal said, "Tonight I mean to have you."

Esther, trembling, rejected the crude proposition.

McNeal leaped to the ground and reached up to help Esther down from the buggy. "Are you coming, girl?"

Esther shook her head, not trusting herself to be able to speak without bursting into tears.

"Don't be so standoffish," McNeal snorted. "You're nothing that special. It's your sister I'd rather get out in the woods."

McNeal's words stung, but his new approach also failed. It was true that Esther was short, stout, and plain compared to her vivacious sister Jenny, but that did not mean that her virture was any easier to come by.

Suddenly McNeal jerked a pistol from his coat pocket and leveled it at Esther's breast. "You'll come with me into the woods, girl," he threatened, "or I'll kill you where you sit."

Esther stared in astonishment. "Don't be a fool, Bob McNeal," she said. Somehow her courage had returned and her amazement at having Bob McNeal threaten her with a pistol turned her fear into anger. "You'll not be buying my honor with a pistol!"

McNeal scalded her with a foul and violent stream of profanity. He cocked the hammer of the pistol, and for a long and terrible moment, Esther wondered if the man might not make good his threat. Then the awful silence was broken by the sound of wagon wheels creaking toward them. A young couple was searching for a quiet spot in the woods to do a little "sparking" before the rain came.

McNeal jammed the pistol back into a pocket, climbed back onto the driver's seat. He looked at Esther just once, his eyes ablaze with anger and wounded pride, then he snapped the reins over the horses' backs and drove them at a breakneck pace back toward the village of Amherst, Nova Scotia.

When Bob McNeal delivered Esther Cox to her door that night, the girl was chilled and drenched to the skin. It had begun to rain on the way home, but, in spite of her pleadings, McNeal had refused to put up the cover of the buggy. It was as if he intended her discomfort to be a punishment for having resisted him.

Never again was Bob McNeal seen in Amherst. He did not report for work at the shoe factory the morning after his attempted seduction of Esther Cox, and his landlady said that he had paid his rent and left.

When Esther learned of McNeal's disappearance, she concluded that the young man must have left town for fear of the consequences if she should tell her brother-in-law, Daniel Teed, of McNeal's threats to her. Daniel had been Bob's foreman at the shoe factory. But she had not told Daniel, nor had she told her married sister, Olive, nor even Jenny. She had bottled up all thought of that terrible night and kept the frightening episode locked tightly in a dark corner of her memory.

Then, one night in January 1879, Esther awakened her sister Jenny with a harsh whisper. "Can you feel something in bed with us?" she asked.

Jenny lay still for a few moments, then jumped from the bed with a scream. "It must be a mouse in the mattress!"

The two sisters beat at the straw of the mattress in an attempt to drive their unwelcome visitor from its hiding place.

"Look there," Jenny said. "See how the straw moves about. It must be trying to make a nest in our mattress."

But as hard as the two girls beat and rustled the straw, they were unable to dislodge any mouse or uncover any sign that one had been in their bed. After watching the mattress for a time and detecting no further movement, the girls concluded that the mouse had escaped without their seeing it.

Jenny suggested that they get back to bed before they awakened the rest of the household. The Cox children—Esther, Jenny, and William—lived with their married sister, Olive, her husband Daniel, their children, and Daniel's brother, John. The two sisters decided to make no mention of their midnight intruder lest they receive a volley of teasing from the two young men in the house.

The next night, however, the girls were awakened by a loud scratching from under their bed. "Mr. Mouse is bound and determined to share our bed," Jenny yawned. "We had better send him packing once and for all."

The sisters lit a lamp, then screamed when a large box filled with quilt scraps jumped out from under the bed. When Jenny stooped to replace the box, it leaped back at her.

Daniel Teed was awakened by the screams and went to investigate. He listened to their story, then, groggily, slid the box of patchwork pieces back under the bed. The box remained immobile. Daniel grumbled something about the bother of women and went back to his room.

The sisters suffered so much mockery from the rest of the household that next day that they dreaded going to bed that night. As it turned out, it would have been better if they had not—especially for Esther.

"I'm dying...I'm dying," she gasped during the night, awakening Jenny.

Jenny turned up the lamp, nearly knocking it off the night table in horror, as she saw the ghastly appearance of her sister.

Esther's complexion had become a bright crimson and her frightened eyes bulged from her skull. Her flesh was hot to the touch and her hair seemed to be standing on end. Most terrifying of all was the sight of her body swelling, as if it were being inflated with air. While Jenny sat stunned at the physical torture her sister was enduring, she became aware of loud thuds which had begun to sound from the walls of their room.

Olive and Daniel were awakened by the noises and appeared at the door of the sisters' room. Olive gave a cry of solicitude and ran to crouch at the side of her younger sister, whose features were becoming more distorted by the moment.

"She's dying," Jenny sobbed. "I know she's dying of some terrible disease!"

There was a particularly loud thud on the wall and Esther's body began to deflate. Within a few moments, her appearance returned to normal.

"But what could have caused such a thing?" Olive wondered aloud.

"Whatever it was," Daniel instruded the women, "we won't say a word of it outside of the household. Is that understood?"

The women agreed that it would be most embarrassing if word got out about Esther's bizarre malady, but secrecy soon became an impossibility.

The next night the sisters' bedclothes became airborne and landed in a heap in a distant corner of the room. Esther's body once again began to swell, and when John Teed entered the room to investigate her terrible moans, a pillow shot from the girls' bed and struck him in the face. Young John retreated and could not be persuaded to re-enter the room. The others sat on the edge of the bed and fought to keep the cover over Esther's swollen and distorted body.

"Here come those thumps again!" Jenny screamed as a thud sounded near her. "They're banging all over the walls, just like last night."

Just as she had the night before, Esther began to deflate after an especially violent series of reports had sounded from the wall above her. Daniel Teed wiped the perspiration from his forehead with the back of a hand. "Tomorrow night we'll be ready for it," he said. "Tomorrow night I'll be fetching Doc Caritte here to see Esther."

Dr. Caritte found himself confronted by something that had not been covered in his medical textbooks. After Esther had prepared for bed, the doctor examined her, and, while he felt her pulse, he remarked that the girl seemed to be suffering from some kind of nervous shock.

The words were scarcely out of the doctor's lips when the girl's pillow puffed itself up as if it were a balloon that had suddenly been filled with air. John Teed grabbed for it, eager for a return bout after the foul blow the pillow had dealt him on the night before. It deflated itself just as soon as the young man grasped it. Then, when Teed stepped back, it re-inflated itself. This time John got hold of it, but it jerked and twisted itself in his arms as if it were a living creature.

While the rest of those assembled had been watching John's weird wrestling match, Jenny Cox was hearing a familiar sound. "Listen," she said, "there's that scratching noise again."

Terror gripped everyone in the room when, as their attention was directed to the scratching, they saw words being etched in the plaster above Esther's head.

"Esther Cox," wrote the invisible hand, "you are mine to kill."

The next evening Dr. Caritte returned with a powerful sedative for Esther.

"I freely admit that this phenomenon is beyond my medical knowledge," the doctor told Daniel Teed. "But since the girl seems to demonstrate certain of the symptoms of nervous excitement, it seems that I might be able to prescribe as I would in similar cases."

Daniel Teed nodded his head. "Then maybe we can all get some sleep, too!"

The sedative had a completely different effect from that for which Dr. Caritte and the family had hoped. The moment Esther was in deep sleep there began on the roof a noise that sounded exactly like someone trying to pound his way into the house with a heavy hammer.

Esther Cox endured such torment for three weeks. Dr. Caritte visited her as often as three times a day making countless unsuccessful attempts to alleviate the girl's suffering. Then one night Esther seemed to fall into a trancelike state and told her secret story of Bob McNeal's attempts to seduce her. Until that moment, not even Jenny had known of Esther's night of fear and temptation.

When Esther regained consciousness, Jenny was at her side to comfort her. "Why didn't you tell me about it?" she asked.

Esther shamefully admitted that the story was true when Jenny told her what she had said in her sleep.

"'I wonder,' Olive said after a moment's reflection, "if Bob McNeal might have been killed or have taken his own life in despair over the terrible thing he tried to do to Esther. Could it be that he has come back to haunt Esther for not giving in to him?"

As if in eager reply, three loud knocks sounded on the bedroom wall.

Jenny and Dr. Caritte quickly devised a simple code, and the "ghost" responded by answering all questions put to him with one rap for "no," two raps for "no answer," and three raps for "yes." The knocking spirit ignored all attempts on Dr. Caritte's part to establish a clue to any previous existence as Bob McNeal.

To Daniel Teed's great embarrassment, the story of the weird happenings in his home could no longer be confined within the family. Neighbors and passers-by had been hearing the strange thuddings for weeks. The Reverend A. Temple of the Wesleyan Methodist Church witnessed a pail of cold water begin to boil when it was set in Esther's presence.

At the time Daniel Teed had called for police protection to keep the curious from trampling his lawn and peering into his windows, Esther came down with diphtheria and all phenomena ceased for the two-week duration of her illness. As soon as she was able to travel, Daniel sent Esther to stay with another of her married sisters for an additional "airing out" of the ghostly manifestations.

Teed never had been particularly sympathetic to his sister-in-law during the onslaught of the phenomena. He seemed more concerned about "what the neighbors would say." Upon Esther's return to his household, he gave Esther and Jenny a new room as an added precaution against any return of the "ghost of Bob McNeal."

Esther had only been home one night when tiny balls of fire began to fall from the ceiling. For three days the household kept a constant vigil against the puffs of flame that drifted about, setting fire to clothing and furniture. Jenny communicated with the invisible firebug through the code system which she and Dr. Caritte had worked out and the ghost told her in blunt terms that it meant to burn down the house.

On the evening of the third day of endless firefighting, Daniel Teed told Esther that raps on the walls were one thing, but fires were something else. He pointed out that if the house caught fire and the wind were just right, half of the town might go up in smoke. He told his sister-in-law that he was sorry, but he could no longer allow her to stay in his home.

Esther was offered employment and lodging by a restaurant owner, John W. White, who theorized that perhaps the girl only needed to get out of the house. But when Esther served customers in his restaurant, the metal utensils leaped from the tables and counters and clung to her body as if she were a living magnet. The furniture shifted about regularly, the heavy door of the kitchen stove refused to stay open, even when braced with an axe handle, and, on one occasion, a fifty-pound box shot fifteen feet into the air.

The well-meaning John White had no choice but to send Esther Cox back to her brother-in-law. The strange manifestations were ruining his business. At that point, Captain James Beck and his wife invited Esther to come to stay with them in their home at St. John, New Brunswick. Captain Beck had read about the "Amherst Mystery" and he was eager to study the phenomena that the newspapers alleged the girl had produced. The Becks invited groups of medical men and scientists to their home to study Esther Cox at their leisure, but Esther proved to be a big disappointment to the investigators who had gathered to psychologically dissect her. For three weeks, the girl did nothing other than relate wild stories of three ghosts which appeared regularly to threaten her with fires and stabbings. The stay at the Beck home was completely devoid of any phenomena, and Esther was politely packed back to Amherst.

Daniel Teed was not yet willing to take a chance with his sister-in-law, but a farmer named VanAmbergh and his wife took the teenager to live with them in the country. Her stay with the VanAmberghs developed into a quiet, pastoral sojourn, and it seemed that the psychic storm had definitely run its course.

At Olive's prodding, Daniel Teed once again welcomed Esther back into the home on Princess Street. The girl had scarcely finished unpacking her bags when the phenomena began with renewed vigor.

Teed was nearly beside himself with anger and confusion. He was a hard-working, uncomplicated man whose sole purpose in life was to provide a decent living for his family and to carve a socially acceptable niche for them in the community. He simply was not psychologically prepared to wage the kind of battle which the ghosts of Esther Cox insisted upon fighting. Church pulpits rang with denunciations of the work of Satan which was being harbored in their midst, and public opinion threatened to drive both Esther and her family from the village.

Teed perhaps would have surrendered to the invisible forces which infected his home if it had not been for the arrival of Walter Hubbell, an American actor and magician. Hubbell, in addition to being a respected actor, had gained some reputation as a debunker of phony spirit mediums. He not only offered to "lay" the ghost that afflicted Esther Cox, but he told Teed that he would pay rent and expenses if he could live in the Teed home and observe the phenomena. Teed found himself unable to refuse the opportunity to get rid of the spook and earn some money all in the same stroke.

Hubbell received a violent reception from the ghost of Bob McNeal on the day he moved in with the Teeds. He had hardly stepped inside the door when his umbrella was jerked from his hand and tossed into the air. A large butcher knife appeared and menacingly zipped through the air to embed itself in the wall beside Hubbell's head.

"I'm afraid Bob and the other ghosts don't like you," Esther said sheepishly.

"Fine," Hubbell said confidently. "Then at least they won't ignore me like they did Captain Beck and his assembled wise men."

At that, every chair in the room fell over with a loud crash. "Wonderful," Hubbell smiled. "Glad to see that everyone is present and accounted for."

Hubbell lived with the Teeds for about five weeks and witnessed almost every conceivable variety of haunting. The furniture always became wildly animated whenever Hubbell entered a room. The ghosts whistled and drummed "Yankee Doodle," and at his request, an invisible trumpet blasted loud enough to set his ears ringing. The instrument finally materialized in quite tangible German silver.

For some reason—perhaps it was his unfailing good nature and confidence—the spirit truly did not seem to "like" Walter Hubbell. Several knives were thrown at him, a large glass paperweight narrowly missed his head, and he suffered innumerable bruises on his limbs wrought by attacking furniture.

Then, as if the ghost of Bob McNeal were jealous of the presence of another male in the house, Esther Cox began receiving more abuse from her invisible tormenter. On one occasion, thirty pins materialized out of the air and sank themselves into difference parts of her body.

Hubbell, the debunker of spiritistic phenomena, found himself totally at a loss to explain the occurrences in the Teed household. But, ever the showman, he began to consider how he might capitalize on Esther Cox's affinity with the ghost of Bob McNeal.

"Think of her on the stage," he said to Daniel Teed. "Put Esther in a loose-flowing black robe, maybe put a few stars and moons on it, then have her put her ghosts through their paces. We could defy any stage magician to duplicate her tricks. Offer a cash reward to anyone who could catch her in a deception. Esther would be a sensation. Soon London, Paris, and Rome would be begging for her."

Hubbell, of course, pointed out that he should serve as her theatrical manager. After all, he did have all the proper connections. Daniel Teed would be a partner in the venture.

"You can't make a public display out of Esther," Jenny objected. "You can't put her on a stage and have the whole world come to gawk at her."

"Daniel, you must not agree to such a thing," Olive Teed begged her husband. "I couldn't bear to see my own sister turned into some kind of a freak."

"But what else is she then?" Daniel Teed demanded. "Is it a normal person who has bangings and thumpings follow him about? Is it a normal person who sets the furniture moving and objects flying through the air?

"Look around at this house," he shouted, indicating the overturned furniture still on the floor after a recent violent seizure. "The place is always in a shambles. How much money have I spent in repairs and in doctor bills since that girl came down with this devil's affliction?

"No," Teed said in a tone of finality, "Esther has caused all this destruction by turning her ghosts loose on this house. It's only fitting and proper that she should do something to pay us back in some way for all the grief she's caused us."

Hubbell rented a large auditorium and sold tickets to curiosity seekers who came from miles around to see the "Wonder of Amherst produce miracles" on the stage. The stage debut of Esther Cox as a professional medium was a complete disaster—the ghosts later blamed the fiasco on Esther's stage fright—and the restive audience was soon chanting, clapping, and demanding the return of their money. Esther was so frightened that, according to the ghosts, she was not able to spare enough psychic energy to allow them to perform their antics. The tour that Hubbell had arranged ended before Esther left Nova Scotia.

Daniel Teed had suffered the proverbial "last straw." He demanded that both Walter Hubbell and Esther Cox leave his house at once. The actor left for St. John, New Brunswick, to write a book on the Amherst mystery, and Esther again sought refuge with the VanAmberghs, who had grown quite fond of the girl during her previous stay with them.

Hubbell's book on the "true ghost story" was published in the latter part of 1879. The book bore signed and notarized affidavits from Olive Teed and sixteen Amherst residents, who swore that Hubbell's account was accurate in every way. By 1916, the book had gone into ten editions.

Esther Cox went to work for a farmer named Davison. After a short period of employment, the girl was arrested as the incendiary responsible for the burning of Davison's barn. When Jenny Cox wrote Hubbell to inform him that Esther had been tried and convicted of the charge, the actor expressed regret that he had not been there to testify on her behalf and to convince the jury that the "ghosts," not Esther, were responsible for the barn burning.

No further manifestations were reported in connection with Esther Cox after the destruction of Davison's barn. She married twice, bore a son from each union, and died in Brockton, Massachusetts, in November, 1912.

As should be clearly in evidence from even a casual reading of the experience of Esther Cox, there is nothing at all romantic about having a "demon lover." The manifestations which afflicted the girl seem plainly psychokinetic in character and appear to have been set in motion by the same kind of sexual shock that sends a poltergeist rampaging about.

An attempted seduction always sets up the Great Question in any young woman's mind; and even though the well-bred, chaste, and cautious conscious of Esther Cox rebuked Bob McNeal for even suggesting such a thing as a romp in the woods, a lusty and uninhibited part of her subconscious would gladly have enjoyed the young man's sexual embrace. The fact that she was plain and more than pleasingly plump no doubt increased the inner pain at her defense of her honor, because Esther was no doubt agonizingly aware that such proposals would not be put to her with a great deal of regularity.

Bob McNeal's disappearance from Amherst, although for what reason no one has ever determined, may have increased the regret that Esther felt and may also have brought on guilt feelings, because, she may have reasoned, the young man must have truly loved her if he left town and his job rather than face her again. It is not known whether Bob McNeal was dead or alive at the time of the onset of the phenomena, but it is not surprising that the ghost was named "Bob."

The masochistic, agent-directed torments suffered by Esther seem to fortify the thesis that her "demon lover" was but a projection of her own psyche, which had been set in motion by her confusion toward sexual matters. The ominous words, "Esther Cox, you are mine to kill," indicate the terrible inner hostility the girl was directing toward her own person.

The role of Daniel Teed in the Amherst mystery is an interesting one to ponder. It seems probable that Esther may have had strongly ambivalent feelings toward her brother-in-law. She seems to have been somewhat frightened of the man and undoubtedly paid him a great deal of respect. Against her conscious wishes she may have felt sexually aroused by living in his house, and she may have increased her feelings of sexual guilt by imagining herself in the role of her married sister, Olive, and therefore vicariously enjoying sex with Daniel Teed. Whether or not such may have been the case, it is noteworthy that Esther produced phenomena in no other home.

There is one notable exception, of course, and that was in Mr. White's restaurant. Here again, in the role of a waitress—one who gives of herself, one who serves—to a predominantly male clientele, Esther may have experienced subconscious sexual conflict.

The arrival of Walter Hubbell, certainly a romantic figure to any small-town girl, was immediately greeted with violent phenomena, which produced as many attacks upon Esther as they did upon the actor. With the exception of some falling furniture which resulted in a few shin bruises, all the knives, paperweights, and other objects went wide of the mark when they were directed at Walter Hubbell. It was the long-suffering Esther who received the pins in her flesh, and on one occasion, a scalp wound when an old bone lifted itself from the yard and struck her on the forehead. Again, it seems that the dashing and confident actor would be most capable of bringing Esther's cauldron of sexual confusion to the boiling point.

With Hubbell out of the village and with herself once again ordered out of her brother-in-law's home, Esther's "ghost" left her, and she readjusted to life with the VanAmberghs. One wonders if it might not have been an unwanted sexual advance on the part of a farmhand that set off the incendiary phenomena that burned down farmer Davison's barn. Although Esther herself was uneducated and unable to write, Hubbell kept in touch with her through Jenny, and never learned of any phenomena after Esther's first marriage.

another eerie thing in the attic

Mrs. Cook was wide awake. The bumping sounds in the attic had stopped, but Mrs. Cook expected them to start again any minute. She pursed her lips and swallowed nervously, waiting for the next thump. But Mrs. Cook was not ready for what happened next.

The wind slammed a branch against the bedroom window. Startled, Mrs. Cook shot her eyes in that direction. When she looked back, a pair of eyes stared at her from the darkness.

"Oh-h-h!" Mrs. Cook's breath almost froze in her throat as she tried to speak.

"Who...who are you? What do you want?"

The eyes glowed menacingly. Mrs. Cook pulled up the covers as they grew larger, coming closer. Then they melted into the darkness. Mrs. Cook breathed easier for a moment but then—thump!

Mrs. Fay Cook's "darned ghost" had resumed his regular habits.

And quite a routine it is. The restless spirit that roams Mrs. Fay Cook's Salt Lake City home at will apparently doesn't care who knows it is there. The thing not only makes things go bump! in the attic at night, but it slams doors, jostles hanging lamps, and drags chairs around the room.

Sometimes the entity does not make use of props, but emits a "funny little sound" all its own. On other occasions, when Mrs. Cook is alone in the house, it lays an invisible, ghostly finger on her arm. If there is an award for not scaring easily, Mrs. Fay Cook must surely qualify.

"I know it sounds strange," admitted the haunted householder to newsman Tom Tiede for NEA. "It's hard for me to believe it all myself. I used to wonder if I was having hallucinations and I tried to figure out natural causes for everything.

"But I don't try to figure them out any more. Too many things happen in this house. I have no doubt that it's really being haunted."

From all appearances, Mrs. Cook is right. Her house's previous owner died in bed twenty-five years ago. According to local legend, a murder had been committed in the neighborhood, and the man was personally connected with both the murderer and his victim.

The impact of the deed apparently was too much for him, and one night he climbed up into a bedroom in the attic, lay down, and closed his eyes to shut out his anguish.

"No one ever heard from him again," says Mrs. Cook. "That is, until recently."

Mrs. Cook is not alone in her opinion that the house is haunted. Mrs. Glenda Christianson, a student of things supernatural, visited the house on a day when the temperature was 90 degrees outside, and experienced "tremendous blasts of cold air" in the attic death room.

There are even spirits who support Mrs. Cook's belief that her house is haunted. A student of self-hypnosis contends that while talking to his deceased Uncle Marvin he was warned to "get the hell out" of the attic bedroom and the house itself. He says that Uncle Marvin's warning also extends to others.

But the clairvoyant and the curious continue to come and go. Falling into both categories was the unidentified young man, who with two friends, entered the house hoping to witness some of its phenomena.

Suddenly his eyes opened wide. He began to stutter and babble incoherently.

"Gr-gr-grgram-m-a! Gr-gr-grand—!"

His companions looked at each other in horror.

"Why's he growling like that?" choked one to the other.

There was no time for a guess. The stricken one began to scream and tear at his clothing. Fearing that he might harm himself, his friends subdued him bodily and dragged him outside.

The youth stopped struggling, and his friends released him.

He sank to his knees on the grass and began to weep. "Grandmother," he kept saying over and over. "I saw my grandmother!" His grandmother had been dead for several years.

The most concrete and most dramatic evidence of the ghost's presence, however, is an exposed sheet of infrared polaroid photographic film. (Infrared film is used to take pictures in total darkness and is capable of capturing images that the human eye cannot see. On Polaroid film, results may be viewed one minute after exposure.)

Hoping to communicate with the restless spirit, Tom Carlin, a Salt Lake City radio personality, entered the attic death room carrying a sheet of such film, factory-wrapped and presealed.

"I was," says Carlin, "very skeptical."

But Tom Carlin emerged a believer. He reported experiencing a number of "strange sensations," one of them an almost stifling odor of bay rum. A search of the house failed to disclose any source for that odor.

Tom Carlin opened the still sealed film package in the presence of his companions. What they saw caused them to gasp and rub their eyes in disbelief. The film was exposed with a shakily written warning: "Danger."

"It's the truth," says Carlin, "so help me!"

But what is truth? Is Mrs. Fay Cook's house really haunted? If the "darned ghost!" is trying to prove his existence, it appears as if he may rest his case. The bumping noises and echoing footsteps, the touches in the dark by invisible fingers, the cold spot, and the spirit writing on the film, are all classic manifestations of the type of haunting known to psychic researchers and Spiritualists as poltergeists, or noisy ghosts.

According to Spiritualistic belief, this type is of a particularly stubborn and defiant nature, generally fond of raising hob in all directions, which operates through the medium of some person's body.

Dr. Nandor Fodor, late psychical researcher and psychoanalyst, believed that poltergeist activity was not so much the work of a discarnate spirit as it was of the haunted one's own personality, related to certain kinds of repression and emotional frustration. But that is not to question the poltergeist's reality.

If Mrs. Cook's "darned ghost" were only a figment of imagination, then what about Mrs. Christianson's cold spot? What of the distraught youth's departed grandmother and "Uncle Marvin's" warning?

In the last analysis, one can only speculate. As Mrs. Fay Cook says: "I realize I can't prove that darned ghost is really here. But on the other hand, nobody can prove that he really isn't!"

To order additional copies of this book,
please send full amount plus $4.00 for
postage and handling for the first book and
50¢ for each additional book.

Send orders to:

Galde Press, Inc.
PO Box 460
Lakeville, Minnesota 55044-0460

Credit card orders call 1–800–777–3454
Phone (612) 891–5991 • Fax (612) 891–6091
Visit our website at http://www.galdepress.com

Write for our free catalog.